Midland Red

MOTORWAY COACHES

NUNEATON · COVENTRY
NON & LONDON STOP
VIA THE MOTORWAY

MIDLAND RED D

MI

Complete Service Daily

		a.m.	p.m.	p.m.
NUNEATON (Bus Station)	dep.	8.00	1.30	6.30
BEDWORTH (Market Place)	dep.	8.10	1.40	6.40
COVENTRY (Pool Meadow)	arr.	8.30	2.00	7.00
COVENTRY (Pool Meadow)	dep.	8.40	2.10	7.10
LONDON (Victoria Coach Station)	arr.	11.00	4.30	9.30

		a.m.	p.m.	p.m.
LONDON (Victoria Coach Station)	dep.	9.00	12.30	7.00
COVENTRY (Pool Meadow)	arr.	11.20	2.50	9.20
COVENTRY (Pool Meadow)	dep.	11.30	3.00	9.30
BEDWORTH (Market Place)	dep.	11.50	3.20	9.50
NUNEATON (Bus Station)	arr.	12.00	3.30	10.00

Fare Table

Daily (except Saturdays, Whitsuntide to end of September)

	Single	Day Return	Period Return
NUNEATON-LONDON - - - -	18/6	25/3	31/-
BEDWORTH-LONDON - - - -	18/-	24/3	29/-
COVENTRY-LONDON - - - -	17/-	23/3	28/-

Saturdays only (Whitsuntide to end of September)

	Single	Day Return	Period Return
NUNEATON-LONDON - - - -	20/6	27/9	33/-
BEDWORTH-LONDON - - - -	20/-	26/9	32/-
COVENTRY-LONDON - - - -	19/6	25/9	31/-

Midland Red
MOTORWAY COACHES

Steve Richards

Midland Red Motorway Coaches
Steve Richards

ISBN 978-0-9563708-1-5

First published in 2010 by
Richards Publishing
48 Longmore Road
Shirley, Solihull, B90 3DY, UK
e-mail: motorwaycoaches@tiscali.co.uk
www.midlandred-motorwaycoaches.co.uk

Printed in England by
Ian Allan Printing Limited
Riverdene Business Park
Molesey Road
Hersham, Surrey
KT12 4RG

Front cover, top: **CM5 4813, on the Coventry-London
service, is on the wind-down into North London.
It is travelling along the concrete-surfaced M10
Motorway, also known as the southern spur. The
photograph was taken in either late-1960 or in
1961.** Ian Allan Library

Front cover, bottom left: **CM5T 4830 was the last
of this variant to remain in service.** Ken Jubb

Front cover, bottom right: **CM6T 5663 spent most
of its working life on the ME2 service.** Omnicolour

Rear cover, top: **The Birmingham-Worcester
service utilised the M5 Motorway and commenced
on the 20th July 1962, the day this motorway
was opened. Photographed in 1964, at Newport
Street, Worcester, is CM5 4833, ready for another
express run to Birmingham.** Martin Llewellyn

Rear cover, bottom: **The only complete BMMO
motorway coach surviving is CM6T 5656; a
resident of the Transport Museum, Wythall.** Author

Title page: **This CM5T has just joined the M1
Motorway bound for London. When this picture
was taken, circa 1963, traffic on the motorway
was still quite sparse.** Ken Jubb

Opposite title page: **A fine period poster, probably
dating from 1962.**

Opposite: **The typical British saloon car could not
compete with the speed of the CM5 coaches.
This photograph is likely to have been taken in
either late 1960 or 1961, on the M1 Motorway
near Leavesden.** Arthur Hustwitt © NA3T

CONTENTS

FOREWORD

The opening of the M1 Motorway in 1959 was an important milestone in the story of road transport in Britain as it helped to make London and the Midlands more accessible, and spearheaded the construction of the network of motorways that have revolutionised the way we move around the country and the time it takes us to get from place to place. More than 50 years ago, travel by car and coach was tedious and time-consuming, so the motorways we take for granted today have done a great deal to make long-distance travel easier and safer.

What is equally remarkable was that the Midland Red company had the foresight to introduce high-speed Birmingham-London links from Day One, and was prepared to design a breed of motorway coaches that would set the standard for some years to come. Suddenly the lightweight coaches favoured by many operators were found to be unsuited to sustained motorway speeds, and the solid, but often-lumbering heavyweight coaches from the main manufacturers were sometimes happier on 'A' roads. And Midland Red moved with the times, producing longer versions of its motorway coaches when the regulations changed. The CM5 and its succes-

sors were truly iconic coaches and their story deserves to be told.

In this impressively-researched book, Steve Richards presents the story of the motorway coaches and the services they provided, but recounts first-hand experiences on the road, including the often apocryphal tales of excessive speed on the M1 Motorway in those days before the 70 mph limit.

Although the distinctive Midland Red coaches disappeared into the relative anonymity of National Express white, there is no doubt that these pioneering routes showed just what could be done to provide better coach links using the growing motorway network.

The Midland Red company itself, lost its West Midlands heartland in 1973, and the rump was carved up in 1981 in preparation for privatisation. However, there is still great affection for Midland Red among former passengers and staff, and among enthusiasts throughout the country, and this book recalls one of the many highlights in the story of the company that grew to be one of the largest and most influential in Britain.

Gavin Booth, Bus and Coach Historian
Edinburgh, Scotland, August 2010

The 2nd November 1959, an historic day for Midland Red. At two o'clock, CM5Ts 4804 and 4809 leave Digbeth with the first fare-paying passengers for the motorway express service. BMMO

PREFACE

My interest in the Midland Red Motorway Coach started with two distinct events. My aunt, who worked at the company offices at Bearwood, knowing of my interest in all things Midland Red, bought me one of the Corgi toy motorway coaches. As a ten-year-old I loved it. Shortly afterwards, my father was doing some building work for a man who I gather was a photographer for Midland Red. On being told of my interest, the man handed over a 10x8 inch yellow Kodak box containing a series of CM5T black and white photos, a motorway express commemorative ticket and a brochure given out on the day the Coventry service was inaugurated.

I never travelled on any of the services undertaken by these motorway coaches. The nearest I got was permission to look inside a CM5T at Bearwood garage in 1964, again my aunt's doing.

My schoolboy interest in Midland Red gave way to one in aviation but in the late 1980s it was rekindled. Having written a number of articles on the motorway coaches during the 1990s, I was invited to assist Corgi with their models of C5 coaches produced in 1/76th scale. As a result, I became quite knowledgeable regarding their outward appearance at least!

With 2009 marking 50 years since the opening of the M1 Motorway and the introduction of Midland Red's first motorway express service, the time was right for a detailed investigation of the complete subject and the volume you are holding is the result. It falls into three sections. The first and longest covers the BMMO C5 class featuring the motorway version. The second part covers the larger, more powerful coaches of the BMMO CM6 class. The final section is made up of a series of related appendices.

Midland Red was more formally known as the Birmingham and Midland Motor Omnibus Co Ltd or BMMO. The titles Midland Red and BMMO are used synonymously. In this book, I have been quite free in using both names. However, I have tended towards BMMO when referring to the bus manufacturing and engineering side, and Midland Red for the operational side. I emphasise the word *tended*, as I have not attempted to be rigorous in this application.

I have been fortunate in having access to good source material and, whilst there are formal acknowledgements elsewhere, I must express here my appreciation to Jim Pearson for his patience and enthusiasm in sharing his wealth of knowledge and experience. The illustrations used include many that will be new to readers, but I have not excluded others simply because they have been seen before.

Hopefully, I have written in an accessible style and not assumed that all of my readers are 'rivet counters' or engineers! I am neither of these and so have sought to understand some of the technical side in order to retell it in lay terms. Extensive use of footnotes has been made in order to maintain the flow of the text and not break up the continuity with lots of numbers and technical detail.

Steve Richards
Solihull, England, August 2010

INTRODUCTION

On Monday 2nd November 1959, the Minister of Transport, Ernest Marples, opened Britain's first motorway.[1] Midland Red was present on day one with the nation's first motorway express coach service, having a specially designed vehicle ready to take on this prestigious role.

With a degree of foresight that had always marked out Midland Red (more correctly the Birmingham and Midland Motor Omnibus Co Ltd) as a leader in its field, the company had seen the possibilities of a non-stop Birmingham-London motorway express service. Such a service would complement the two existing intermediate stop services, one which routed through Daventry and Dunstable (route code G) and the other through Bicester and Aylesbury (route code J), each taking some 5 hours 20 minutes. As early as 1st October 1958, the company applied for the necessary Road Service Licences for the new route, which were eventually granted. Meanwhile, the BMMO design team proceeded to work on the project which would give birth to the CM5 high-speed motorway coach.

Midland Red's CM5 and CM6 class motorway coaches generated a great amount of interest, both from within the industry and outside it. The engineering, styling and high speeds first seen with the introduction of the CM5 coaches, combined with the public's awe for those privileged to drive them, produced a sense of elitism amongst all staff connected with these vehicles and ensured that the name Midland Red shone brightly.

Rumours and stories, spoken in hushed voices, soon circulated about the speeds being attained on motorway services and

Notes

1 This was designated the M1. Strictly speaking the Preston by-pass was the first insofar as it was built to motorway standards. This road was not given an M number and subsequently was incorporated into the M6 Motorway. See Appendix G.

timings for journeys between England's first and second cities which were being progressively shaved. Coaches were said to be doing the 'ton', and for the first seven years of operation that would have been perfectly legal. Even after 1967, when a 70 mph limit was introduced it was not enforced with vigour. In fact, the police seemed to have an understanding with the motorway coach drivers, acknowledging that both parties were respected professional drivers and could be trusted not to do anything foolish.

In later years, some have doubted the validity of such stories, believing them to be folklore built up through their retelling. But there's no smoke without fire. Lloyd Penfold drove CM6Ts shortly before their withdrawal from service and gives us this account:

'I could manage the 120-mile London run in under 2 hours easily, usually 1 hour 50 minutes, occasionally in 1 hour 40 minutes. What would have been the fastest trip though, was marred by being stopped by an irate policeman. It was like this...

'I often would do, on a Friday evening, a duplicate journey to the 18:00 London service, scheduled to return from Victoria at 21:30. However, once in Victoria Coach Station, I would volunteer myself to the duty inspector to stay back and duplicate the 23:00 Manchester service, taking the Birmingham and sometimes Coventry passengers, which would allow more seats to be sold for passengers travelling further north. Back in the mid-to-late 1970s Londoners would be in bed by ten o'clock, and the roads out of the capital were

fairly clear. The M1 was empty at that time of night too, so a spirited run could be made.

'On this particular night I'd judged the Edgware Road traffic lights well, and was on the motorway in 17 minutes. The CM6 I had went very well. Once on the M6 and past Coventry (no passengers for there on this occasion), there was hardly any other traffic on the road. Packington bank came and my foot stayed down for the descent. The only other vehicle northbound was behind me, its headlights indicating it was about a quarter of a mile back. Once down the bank, approaching Coleshill, the speed dropped slightly and the headlights behind gradually caught me up. Just at the Castle Bromwich exit it passed me and I could see it was a Triumph 2000 police car, white with a reflective red stripe along the side. It was blowing a bit of blue smoke I noticed. On came the blue light and we stopped just by Fort Dunlop. The copper jumped from the car, not even stopping to put on his hat. He approached the coach, pulled open the front door.

'He jabbered, "Do you know how fast you were going?"

I replied, "Of course not, the speedo only goes up to eighty."

"Down Packington bank," he gasped, "I was doing a hundred and I wasn't catching you."

"Yes," I replied, smiling weakly, "these are fast, aren't they?" After listening to him rant about how coaches shouldn't go that fast, he let me go. I checked my watch as I pulled into Digbeth – quarter to one, and he'd stopped me for nearly ten minutes. Curses!'

Restyled CM6T 5657, in its National Bus Company (NBC) white livery, is seen heading south on the M6 Motorway. T W Moore

PART ONE

Speeding
into the *1960s*

The BMMO C5, CM5T, CM5, CS5 and C5A

CM5T 4807 shows well the various external modifications introduced on this class; twin headlamps, raised bumper, two roof lights and white-painted roof panel. It is heading north on the M1 Motorway in September 1963. Ken Jubb

POST-WAR LINEAGE

The years following the end of the Second World War were ones of hardship and shortages. To keep their spirits up, young women could turn to Christian Dior's 'New Look' (1947). Those young men enthused by modern public transport, especially Midland Red transport, had a 'new look' also, one to brighten the austere days.

BMMO had not been idle during the war years and were set to introduce new looking vehicles just as soon as manufacturing capacity would allow. The main effort was directed towards the new underfloor-engined series of single-decker buses, the S6, S8 and S9 (1946-1949). The D1 double-decker of 1944, with its full-width bonnet, concealed radiator and rear entrance, gave its stylish body design to the AD2 class (1949-1950) which utilised an AEC Regent II chassis.

As if all of these new-look buses weren't enough, a new coach based on the S6 bus was introduced in 1948. It had an eye-catching 30-seat body which, like the other new Midland Red vehicles, was designed by the company but was contracted out to a specialist coachbuilder for manufacture. In the case of the 45 C1 coaches, this was Duple. In 1950, a further 12 coaches for Midland Red's famous long-distance 'coach cruises' were built. Designated C2, these were similar to the C1 but obvious differences included the fact that both front windscreens were recessed; the centrally-positioned entrance door was hinged and not sliding; the driver's offside door was dispensed with, as was his separate cabin, and the seating was reduced from 30 to 26 for added passenger comfort.

Coach development moved forward again in 1953 when BMMO's Central Works at Carlyle Road, Edgbaston, Birmingham, turned

Above left: **During the war years, BMMO had experimented with underfloor-engined single-decker buses. This work resulted in the S6 type. Fleet number 3000 was the first and entered service in October 1946.** BMMO

Above right: **The BMMO D1 double-decker was built in 1944 and looked very modern with its full-width bonnet and concealed radiator.** BMMO

Right: **The first BMMO post-war coach was the C1. Based on the S6 chassis, it had an attractive body designed by the company in conjunction with Duple.** Author

out a new prototype. This was to the newly approved 30ft long by 8ft wide design dimensions and was, in essence, an enlarged C1. The attractiveness of this coach seems to have been overlooked but it was perhaps more aesthetically pleasing than the famous Burlingham Seagull of that period. The windscreens were now fixed, flat but rounded at the corners; full-width wrap-around bumpers were located at the front and back, and a polished aluminium trim fitted over the wheel arches was a nice touch. This prototype was allocated fleet number 4242 (registration UHA 242) and had 32 seats and roof quarter lights, it being intended for long-distance coach cruises. In 1954, the coachbuilder Alexander used this vehicle as a pattern and produced a further 11. These were designated the C4 class. The C3 class, for standard coaching work, was built in 1954 and could be readily identified by its lack of roof quarter lights. Each of the 63 coaches had 37 seats and the bodies for the class were built by Willowbrook.

ENTER THE C5

In 1958, Midland Red unveiled the latest in its series of post-war coaches, the C5. It was based on the current single-deck bus then being produced by BMMO. This bus was built to two specifications, the S14 and S15, the latter being dual-purpose, suitable for long distance stage-work and coaching. Midland Red had designed and built the majority of its own vehicles since 1923, although outside bodybuilders were used for production batches. The S14 was the first bus to be completely built in-house. Again it was to the 30ft long and 8ft wide dimension, with a 44-seat layout. It was of integral construction (known as monocoque, dispensing with the traditional steel chassis frame) and made use of light alloy and fibreglass on the outer panels. BMMO's pioneering work and continual development of fibre-reinforced polymer resulted in later-production S14s having a one-piece moulded roof. Body framework was supplied by Metal Sections Ltd.[2] The company's horizontal underfloor version of the 'KL' 8.028 litre engine[3] was fitted, which drove single rear wheels on a Kirkstall[2] 4.78:1 ratio hypoid bevel axle, via a David Brown[2] 4-speed constant mesh gear-

box. Girling[2] hydraulically operated disc brakes, with Lockheed[2] constant flow servo-assistance, were fitted to all four wheels. The handbrake also was of the disc type, operating on the transmission. Metalastik[2] variable rate[4] rubber suspension was used at the back and front, with each of the front wheels being sprung independently. The result was a unique lightweight bus of just over 5 tons. The family resemblance of these vehicles would remain evident through to the last S23 class delivered in 1970.

Production spanned 1954-1959 and many variations were apparent within the 219 produced. The dual purpose version, the S15, was built as a 40-seater and had a deeper windscreen, with alterations to the front roof dome and route indicator box; a small luggage compartment at the rear; twin back wheels; Auster[2] hopper ventilators and polished aluminium mouldings. Extensive use of glass fibre meant the bus weighed in at 5 tons 19 cwt. The S15 was painted in coach livery – red with black roof – and was produced in two batches, 50 in 1957 and a further 48 in 1962.

It was the last numbered S14, 4722 (722 BHA), which was actually completed as the C5 prototype. Like the S15, it had twin wheels at the rear but otherwise was mechanically similar to its bus origin. It had a completely redesigned front and rear end. The back featured curved corner perspex windows (curved windows having first appeared on the front end of the C3/C4 coaches), a baggage compartment with a top-hinged balanced door and an offside emergency door complete with folding step. At the front end, the new radiator grille was topped by a somewhat bland-looking two-piece curved windscreen, which gave the

Above: **The C4 coach with its centrally-positioned destination box, wraparound bumper, wheel arch trim and curved windows was a hint of things to come. Fleet number 4242 was built entirely at BMMO's Central Works, Edgbaston, Birmingham.** BMMO

Left: **In the early 1960s, the motorway coach would be presented to youngsters in toy form and in the *Eagle* comic. A decade earlier, a pocket sized children's story book, *By Coach to the Seaside*, featured a coach based squarely on Midland Red's C1. It was published by Birn Brothers of London.**

Notes

2 Body frame, gearbox, axles, braking system, suspension and the ventilation system although made by specialist manufacturers, were either completely to BMMO design specifications or were joint developments for BMMO use.

3 The normal vertically orientated 'KL' engine had first been used in the BMMO D7 double-decker lightweight bus, which entered service in 1953.

4 'Variable rate' refers to the degree of deflection available staying near constant whether the vehicle is unladen, partly laden or fully laden.

The S14 was a revolutionary 44-seat lightweight bus. It was of integral construction, fitted with rubber suspension, disc brakes and some fibreglass was used in the bodywork. The S14 class vehicles were the first to be built entirely at the newly expanded Central Works, without recourse to outside bodybuilders. BMMO

The S15 was the dual-purpose version of the S14. It had 40 seats and twin wheels were fitted to the rear axle. 5073 was part of a second batch completed in 1962, and is seen here in service at the Transport Museum, Wythall, in July 2007. Author

driver problems with reflections from the interior lighting. The solution turned out to be the type's distinguishing feature, the now classic 'lantern' windscreen. The roof was fibreglass, with a centrally-positioned roof extractor vent at the rear. Fibreglass was used on the body wherever practicable, i.e. for curved panels, side inspection covers, wheel arches and boot door. The front roof dome housed the centrally-mounted destination box. The entrance door opened outwards and was the first BMMO-designed coach to have the entrance forward of the front axle. With full-width wrap-around bumpers front and rear, and tasteful use of polished aluminium moulding, the vehicle was both attractive and unique.

Passenger comfort was a high priority for the design team. Particular attention was given to ventilation. Above each saloon window was an Auster hopper ventilator. With this open, fresh air entered and, with the use of blanking strips, was directed over the top of the

Photographed in early 1958 is 4722, the prototype C5 coach. This offside view clearly shows the rear window and emergency door arrangement peculiar to the prototype. Transport Museum, Wythall collection

Again seen in early 1958 is the prototype C5 coach. It has the original windscreen which was soon replaced by the now familiar 'lantern' windscreen. BMMO

The rear window framing style of the prototype 4722 would be modified when the type entered production. BMMO

parcel racks, so avoiding unwanted direct air flow. During the summer months, the blanking strips could be removed and the welcome breeze would enter the saloon beneath the parcel racks. In addition, there were two air-intake flaps above the windscreen, in the roof dome, which were manually controlled from inside the vehicle. Each of these was paired to a two-speed fan. These bulkhead fans, which were controlled by the driver, could be used to force the inducted air across the ceiling above the parcel racks. The roof-mounted extractor fan at the rear completed the operation. This system was available to ensure a good movement of air when the coach was slow-moving or stationary. Clearing the atmosphere, in the days when many passengers smoked tobacco, was necessary. Heating came from three Clay-

Notes

5 Overly warm interiors became a problem. Early in 1959 two opening roof lights were tested but not fitted to production vehicles until much later. When they were, the top of the roof was also painted white to reflect the sun's heat.

6 This was fitted despite the fact the development department had established that a fully laden S15 with its higher ratio axle could not pull away on a hill steeper than 1:6.

ton Dewandre units, positioned beneath the seats, with demisters to the front windscreen.

Soundproofing was aided by filling the cavity between the inner and outer roof skins with sewn fibreglass sheeting, which also doubled as insulation.[5] The 37 seats were in a multi-coloured floral moquette and had individually adjustable headrests and ashtrays. The first production model (and possibly others) also had newspaper holders mounted on the seat backs together with a chrome-plated grab rail. A two-position footrest was also provided. The driver sat enclosed only by a waist high partition which opened outward, towards the passenger door. There was no offside driver's door.

The prototype 4722 was on the road in April 1958. In accordance with a recommendation from the development department, it was using a 4.44:1 rear axle ratio,[6] like that of the S15. This was short-lived and by the time it was allocated to Digbeth garage the following month, it had the 4.78:1 rear axle. A production

batch of 64 was hot on its heels. The first of these was delivered to Bearwood in August 1958 and then various garages received them through the remainder of the year but most were delivered in 1959. The last few arrived on the scene in early 1960. These coaches had the 4.78:1 differential from new; the rear end of the body was redesigned to provide for a wider emergency door; the rear-end window framing was reshaped; the roof was now a single piece fibreglass moulding and the destination box was now slanted downwards for easier viewing.

For all of its good looks and passenger comfort, the coach was not impressive with its sedate performance. It had retained the S14 4-speed gearbox and 8.028 litre engine but, with the lower differential ratio axle, drivers considered its performance inferior to the C3/C4 class. Later it will be seen that many of these standard C5 coaches were mechanically upgraded.

BMMO often considered design features, sometimes including them on prototypes or as one-offs on standard vehicles. These could be set to one side only to reappear many years later. This sketch dates from 1949 and shows a proposed front entrance for the C1 coach. When the C5 appeared nearly 9 years later, it was the first BMMO-designed coach to have a forward passenger entrance.

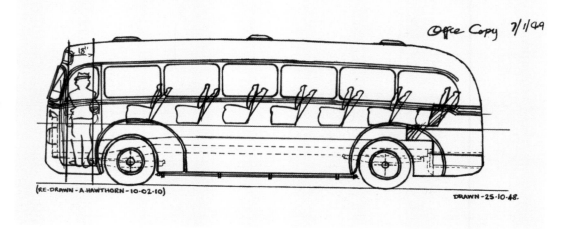

(RE-DRAWN - A.HAWTHORN -10-02-10)   DRAWN -25-10-48.

Top left: The moquette on the passenger seats was of a floral design. Note the string net newspaper holder, most likely only on 4774. BMMO

Top right: 4778 is parked with the driver's windscreen open. Although opening windscreens had been a legal obligation for many years, vehicles like the C5 which had demisters were actually exempt. Surfleet Transport

Left: There were two long-distance routes from Birmingham to London, one via Aylesbury and the other via Daventry. 4783 is seen on the latter. Andrew Hawthorn collection

Below left: A C5 under construction in Central Works. BMMO

Below right: The rear end of a C5 under construction. Chris Hodge Trucks Neg no. aaw061

This page:

C5 4785 on a trip to The Mumbles, Swansea, in early autumn 1959.
Ken Jubb

4788 leaving Birmingham bound for one of the 'Brummies' favourite seaside resorts, Llandudno. R H G Simpson

Seen in April 1959 at the Red Lion terminus in Stratford-upon-Avon, is C5 4783 on a half-day tour. The Stratford Blue double-decker is JUE 357, a Leyland PD2 built in 1950.
John Senior

Opposite page:

Rear window framing was modified after the first few C5s were built.
Fig. 1 represents the initial design but most were as Fig. 2; Early C5s had a roof ventilator similar to the majority of S14s. This was soon modified as seen on Fig. 3; The vertical radiator grille moulding came in two forms. These are illustrated in Fig.4. The left one represents earlier production vehicles.

This 'snap' of 4798 was taken at the small city of Wells, Somerset, in April 1960. This is possibly its first outing, having been delivered to Sutton Coldfield garage that month. Transport Museum, Wythall collection

Typical autumn tours leaflet from 1965.

4818 spent most of its coaching life at Kidderminster, arriving there in April 1961, and 4820, of a similar age, was at Cradley Heath for most of its early service.
Photobus

FIG 1

FIG 2

FIG 3

FIG 4

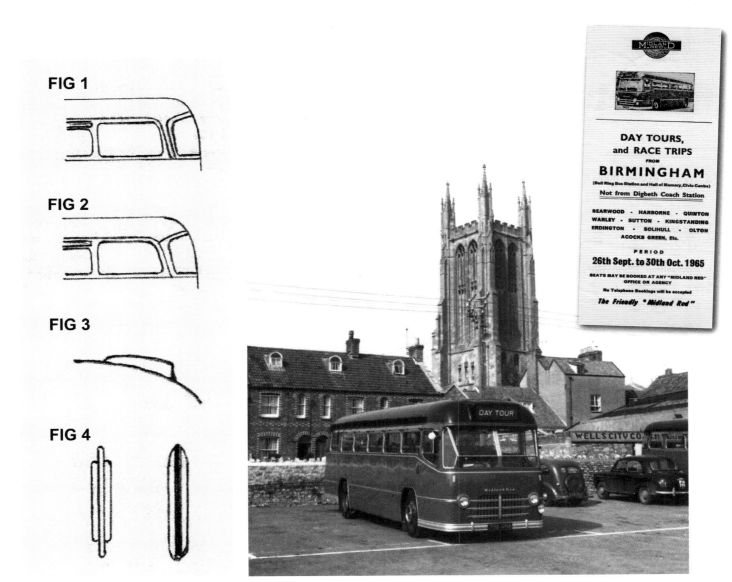

HIGH-SPEED DEVELOPMENT

In April 1959, it was confirmed that there would be no speed restrictions placed upon coaches operating on the new motorways. At a similar time Road Service Licences were awarded to Midland Red following their application made on 1st October of the previous year. The M1, together with the M45 northern spur and the M10 southern spur, would be opened before the new decade commenced. BMMO General Manager, Donald Sinclair, gave Development Engineer, Jim Pearson and his team of Technical Assistants the task to develop a high-speed motorway coach capable of a reliable and sustained top speed of 80 mph. For obvious practical reasons, the newly introduced C5 coach was used as the basic vehicle to be upgraded. Some 50 years on, Jim Pearson recalls that he was given a free hand with no budget restrictions. Initially three Technical Assistants formed part of the development team but this figure increased so that by mid-1960 there were no fewer than eight Technical Assistants involved at different stages. Jim says, 'At times it was a job in itself to keep them all usefully employed.'

Fleet number 4796 (796 GHA) was withdrawn uncompleted from the assembly programme at Central Works and used as an experimental vehicle. It was painted in overall green primer and, where fitted, the polished aluminium trim was still covered over in protective material. The destination box aperture still had not been cut out and interestingly the coach had two roof lights, a feature which would not appear again on this class of coach until 1963.

To meet the requirements of a coach suitable for a motorway express service, notable changes were introduced by the BMMO designers. Although the C5 standard coach had not excited the men who drove it, on account of its bus-like performance, the design was more than sound and would readily lend itself to the forthcoming pioneering role. Steering, braking and suspension were ready for the new task with no compromise on safety, although it is true that the rear rubber suspension was to be stiffened by use of heavier damper settings. With its existing gearbox and rear axle, the 98 bhp of the C5 coach gave a top speed of 48 mph.[7] Test bed work led BMMO engineers to the conclusion that they would need something in excess of 130 bhp together with an increase in engine maximum revs to meet the proposed requirement of 80 mph. Various turbochargers were tried and a BSA[8] Type 12 model was adopted as it was of a more compact design, bearing in mind the limited space available when the engine was installed. Superchargers of the day, as used on sports and racing cars, were mechanically driven from the engine. The turbocharger in the 1950s was to a relatively simple design comprising a turbine driven by the exhaust gases, which was connected via a shaft to a compressor turbine. This then

Notes

7 48 mph maximum speed was achievable at 1800 rpm, using the fourth gear ratio of 1:1 and the final drive (rear axle) ratio of 4.78:1.

8 CAV had recently taken over this product.

9 3 inches was on the generous side to reduce back pressure below 1.5 inches of mercury.

10 L.G. Wyndham Shire was Chief Engineer at BMMO 1912-1940.

11 'Overdrive' is when the number of engine revolutions is lower than the revolutions turned by the propeller shaft entering the differential. Normally, a gearbox reduces the revolutions by lessening degrees as the gear ratio increases. First gear has the most reduction and top gear is normally at a ratio of 1:1 (known as 'direct'). In the case of the CM5, the overdrive ratio was 0.73:1. Thus 0.73 of an engine revolution turned the propeller shaft at the back of the gearbox one full turn and then the 4.44:1 rear axle gearing reduced this again, making for an overall ratio of 3.24:1 i.e. 324 turns of the engine = 100 turns of the wheels.

The BMMO Type S14 8 litre Engine with CAV Turbocharger

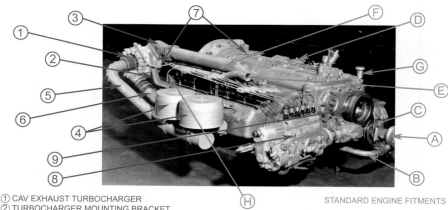

① CAV EXHAUST TURBOCHARGER
② TURBOCHARGER MOUNTING BRACKET
③ EXHAUST ADAPTOR PIPE
④ TWO COOPER'S PAPER ELEMENT AIR FILTERS
⑤ FILTER AIR FEED PIPE TO TURBOCHARGER
⑥ PRESSURED AIR PIPE TO ENGINE VIA CAST-IN AIR DUCTS IN ROCKER COVERS
⑦ AUXILARY OIL FEED PIPE TO TURBOCHARGER (PAPER ELEMENT FILTER AND OIL DRAIN FROM TURBOCHARGER TO ENGINE NOT SHOWN)
⑧ UPRATED CAV "B" TYPE FUEL PUMP
⑨ METALASTIK CRANKSHAFT DAMPER

STANDARD ENGINE FITMENTS

Ⓐ WATER PUMP
Ⓑ WATER FEED PIPE TO ENGINE
Ⓒ BEVEL DRIVE FROM CAMSHAFT TO FUEL PUMP
Ⓓ GLACIER CENTRIFUGAL OIL FILTER
Ⓔ WATER OUTLET PIPE
Ⓕ EXHAUST MANIFOLD
Ⓖ ENGINE CRANKCASE BREATHER
Ⓗ INJECTOR DRIBBLE RETURN PIPE

compressed the air entering into the engine inlet manifold. When this air mixed with the increased quantity of fuel injected into the combustion chamber, the extra volume of the resulting combustion provided the additional energy needed. To ease the installation of the turbocharger and in view of the limited space available, the existing exhaust manifold was retained, this being linked to the turbocharger via a short adaptor pipe. This was more than adequate for the job even if the turbocharger response was reduced a little. One minor drawback was the emission of black smoke, which occurred if the driver accelerated hard whilst the engine speed was low.

A happy spin-off from the use of the turbocharger was the quietening effect it had on exhaust noise. The 3-inch diameter[9] straight-through exhaust system required no silencer, just an open expansion box to keep exhaust noise at reasonable levels.

At this point the name Arthur Parkes should be mentioned. This gifted craftsman was a member of the development team and had worked for Midland Red for many years, going back to the days of L.G. Wyndham Shire.[10] He was involved in the engine bench tests of the CM5 turbocharged engine and he made all the necessary components that were required to mount the turbocharger, oil filter and air cleaners onto the 8.028 litre engine.

Testing would eventually yield a top speed of 85 mph, using a BMMO-specified David Brown 5-speed gearbox – the fifth gear being over-drive.[11] It was necessary to have a 'faster' rear axle, so the Kirkstall 4.44:1 ratio axle was used.

Contrary to popular perception, the addition of the turbocharger was not simply to attain a high maximum speed, but to secure a good acceleration. It was necessary to have a sufficient reserve of power to overtake other vehicles in a minimum distance and to manage the motorway's 1 in 30 gradients at a reasonable speed. By the time the motorway service began, good acceleration was indeed achieved, with 70 mph being reached in 70 seconds, fully laden. This meant that good timings for services could be had without pushing the coaches to their limits. Travelling flat out with a full load would, due to wind resistance, incur the penalty of increasing fuel consumption considerably, from around 15 mpg to 10 mpg.

In either late March or early April and after 'running in' for 500 miles, the prototype was tested at the Motor Industry's Research Association (MIRA)[12] Proving Ground at Lindley, near Nuneaton. The coach was taken on to the 2.8-mile circuit where the speed was allowed to build up in stages to a maximum of 73 mph, the 70 mph mark being reached in 94 seconds. The coach remained stable and the steering positive, whilst the brakes were more effective than they were at slower speeds (see footnote 31 on page 35). Jim says, 'As the nominated target was 80 mph, we had taken the precaution of bringing the Fuel Pump Shop Foreman, Jim Dougall, along with us to make any fur-

Notes

12 The CM5 was the first heavy vehicle officially allowed on the high-speed circuit.

4796 was used as a test vehicle for the CM5 development work. It was photographed at the MIRA Proving Ground in March or April 1959. The vehicle is in green primer and most of the trim is masked, a discarded destination blind being used for masking on the bumper! Jim Pearson is at the wheel, and just visible are Peter Wood (Assistant Engineer), Ken Worrall (Technical Assistant) and Jim Dougal (Fuel Pump Shop Foreman).
Photo via Jim Pearson

Notes

13 Mileages for the CM5 prototype were: End of April 1959, 1,350; end of June 1959, 6,414; end of August 1959, 10,029.

14 The top land of the pistons was reduced to the extent of 0.004 inch tapering and the skirt was relieved to the extent of 0.001 inch.

ther adjustments to the fuel pump. He therefore altered the stop to the fuel rack, allowing extra fuel to be delivered, also adjusting the fuel pump governor springs to increase the maximum engine rpm. After a couple of further test runs and an extra tweak to the fuel pump, we achieved the magical figure of 80 mph, timed over a measured half mile.'

There were 10,000 miles of test runs made.[13] Continuous high-speed running was done to check engine temperatures, transmission and tyres. Brake tests involved slowing from 70 mph to 30 mph every 90 seconds; this was kept up for 2 hours with no drop in efficiency of the Girling brakes. Another brake-fade test involved slowing from 60 mph to 20 mph three times on every circuit of the MIRA track. This was done continuously for three hours with no significant fade.

As motorway operation was new to the UK, there was much speculation regarding traffic flow and possible congestion. Some believed that it would be possible to drive the length of the motorway without touching the brakes. Others were concerned that there would be both congestion caused by slow-moving overtaking lorries and hold-ups due to the volume of traffic. Brake tests at MIRA were designed to cover all scenarios.

During August, after the 10,000 miles of extensive testing of the prototype, the coach passed to the bodyshop for fitting out and major running components were stripped down for examination. As a result, modification to the engine pistons was made.[14]

Ex-Midland Red employee Bob Richards, who was one of the Technical Assistants, recalls some of the incidents associated with the high-speed trials: 'On tests, we found all sorts of things were going wrong. We suddenly blew an engine and found the duplex chain, which came off the crankshaft and drove the oil pump and camshaft, wasn't man enough for the job. We had to make a triple chain.'

Jim Pearson recalls this happening around May or June, on the very day the General Manager, D.M. Sinclair, was travelling over to MIRA to have his first drive of the coach. He would have to wait some weeks before he got behind the wheel for his high-speed run. Jim explains, 'The engine failure, as described by Bob Richards, was not unexpected. We just didn't know at what point it would fail. It had been known for several years that the 8-litre engine had a bad crankshaft torsional vibration at engine revolutions around 2,100 rpm, and during our engine bench tests with the turbocharged engine this was confirmed. As a result, Metalastik were involved in engine tests to provide a suitable damper which would resolve the problem. It was also decided to adopt a belt-and-braces approach by fitting a Triplex Chain drive in place of the normal Duplex set-up. Unfortunately, neither of these units was immediately available and, in view of the tight time schedule, it was considered essential that the high-speed testing at MIRA should start as soon as possible.'

Bob continues, 'There were various things like windscreen wipers blowing off the screen which were fixed by fitting stronger springs. Later we had to fit screen washers, but the washer fluid didn't even touch the screen at 85 mph – you could see it going over the roof. Eventually, Lucas provided some high-pressure washers and we used those.'[15]

The C5 body had a frontal area of 85 square feet and had not been designed with streamlining in mind. One factor of speeds in excess of 60 mph is wind resistance, which is indicated by wind noise. Bob Richards says, 'By the time the coaches entered service, the most wind noise was being caused by the protruding hinges of the outward-opening passenger door. In the end, we quietened them by fitting small metal plate deflectors forward of the hinges.'

Engineers had to wait until the service on the motorway itself started before a proper assessment of the tyres could begin because testing at MIRA was not representative. Jim Pearson again, 'Initially we looked to Dunlop as they were an international company and we assumed that they would have experience in operating high-speed heavy vehicles in the USA and Germany. It was left to them and the other major tyre suppliers to Midland Red, namely Firestone and Goodyear, to make the appropriate enquiries but they all drew a blank. As a result, we and the UK-based tyre companies were in uncharted waters regarding the high-speed testing of tyres. The problem was not helped by the MIRA circuit which, despite the banking on the curved portions of the track, still put abnormal loads on the offside tyres, especially the front one.'

On one such test run at MIRA, the front offside tyre suddenly burst whilst the coach was travelling at 70 mph. What might have been a nasty incident, in fact turned out fine. The coach remained controllable and was brought safely to rest. Apart from the tyre, only the two offside front panels sustained damage.

Jim continues, 'After the tyre blow-out incident, we were obliged to limit the number of high-speed circuits and interpose a number of low-speed runs to cool down the tyres. By September 1959, we were using the Dunlop RB6 radial ply tyre. Up until that time, we had been using standard heavy-vehicle commercial tyres, not the ones used on public transport vehicles which had a thicker tread.'

On a visit to MIRA in Summer 1959, BMMO's General Manager got his run, making 82 mph.[16] He had overseen all of BMMO's wartime development work and the subsequent introduction of numerous new types into the company's fleet, but this occasion must have topped them all.

At the start of September, Midland Red officially announced details of its new coach and the forthcoming motorway express service. The press release photo purported to show Donald Sinclair's coach on the banked track at MIRA. The picture is most interesting, in that it shows the test coach with two skylights and twin headlights. Jim Pearson has noted that they did indeed run the prototype coach with twin headlights as early as May/June, although this innovation would not see the light of day on motorway coaches for at least 18 months.

The press coverage made the national and local newspapers, radio, and both BBC and ITV television, with camera units being sent to Central Works. Further interest was generated when, in the same week, the government announced that the M1 Motorway would open on 2nd November.

Notes

15 The screen washers were first fitted in November 1959 after service operation commenced. Although the only screen washer available was a private car fitment, initial driver's reports were favourable. Later a larger container was mounted near the radiator to make the topping-up of water easier for the driver.

16 To make this speed, it was found necessary for a vehicle to have completed 1,500 miles by which time running units were deemed properly bedded in.

In either July or August, General Manager, Donald Sinclair, drove the test coach at over 80 mph. By this stage the front panel had been replaced and featured twin headlamps. BMMO

The first production CM5T was 4801, and it was used at MIRA from August 1959, this picture being taken a month later. BMMO

Two rear views of 4801. The toilet compartment meant that the luggage space was reduced by 20%. (On the later CM6T, which had ten more seats, limited boot space would be viewed with dismay by the Traffic Department.) Note the two extractor vents on the roof; a single centrally positioned vent was used on non-toilet variants. BMMO

The fitted carpet and leopard-skin moquette gave the CM5T interior a plush look. BMMO

Production CM5T 4803 on the high-speed track at MIRA. Technical Assistant, Trevor Yeo, is driving.
Photo via Jim Pearson

Looking like a couple of Corgi models, two CM5Ts at MIRA. BMMO

The first production motorway coach 4801 (801 HHA) was available for testing at MIRA around the same time that the prototype's work finished. It was designated CM5T (<u>C</u>oach <u>M</u>otorway <u>5</u> type class <u>T</u>oilet). 4801 would be much publicised in the following few months. The most obvious interior feature was the inclusion of a toilet compartment at the rear nearside, although this reduced the seating capacity from the C5's 37 to 34 and reduced the boot space somewhat. The toilet compartment was built at the company's Central Works, using a two-section fibreglass moulding. The toilet was of the chemical type and a wash basin was installed with a gravity water tank that held 12 gallons. Access was through a sliding door (later coaches were fitted with a hinged door). The lock was coupled to a lamp to signify when it was engaged. A mirror and towels completed the convenience. Inclusion of the toilet compartment meant that the roof extractor-fan was moved from its centreline

position to the offside, and a second extractor was fitted to the nearside, above the toilet compartment.

Like the C5, the interior was peony and white, but the seating was covered in a striking leopard-skin[17] moquette. Fitted carpet was laid over the half-inch plywood floor adding to the sense of luxury and doubtless aided the existing soundproofing. The side lining panels were finished in a nylon/rayon fabric. Interior lighting was provided above each window pillar and along the ceiling centreline.

In closing this section, it is interesting to relate the following 'mystery': At the time, some in engineering circles had expressed surprise at the high speeds these motorway coaches were reaching, in view of their modest power/weight ratio and unstreamlined body shape. This matter was mentioned in a technical paper presented by the Development Engineer, Jim Pearson, in March 1962, at

Notes

17 In an article written by D. M. Sinclair in May 1961, the General Manager refers to this as jaguar skin.

Nostalgic view of High Street, Digbeth with St Martin's in the Bull Ring in the background. CM5T 4809 is on a road test coming out of Smithfield Street. A Birmingham Corporation Leyland PD2, with Brush body, waits at the traffic lights.
Chris Hodge
Trucks Neg no. aax275

a time when each of the CM5Ts had completed about 150,000 miles.

The paper showed that the power requirement to drive the coach, as calculated from coasting deceleration tests, amounted to 189 bhp[18] at 80 mph. Yet maximum recorded output on the test bed was about 135 bhp. The paper acknowledged that this large discrepancy could not be explained! The matter was resolved just recently, when Jim Pearson met with Dick Nutt. Dick had worked as a Technical Assistant with Midland Red up

to the mid-1950s, but was working for Ford by the time the CM5 came on the scene. It turns out that Ford, mainly for their own interest, offered to carry out some testing during BMMO's own development period. Jim recalls, 'Actually, I wasn't too bothered one way or the other about this, as we'd got the result we wanted – an 80 mph coach.' It was Ford who came in with the calculation of 189 bhp. Dick confessed to Jim when they met a couple of years ago, that Ford had got their sums wrong.

The BMMO CM5T Motorway Coach

Notes

18 This theoretical figure reckoned on 122 bhp to overcome air resistance, tyre drag accounted for 52 bhp and transmission losses 15 bhp.

19 These consisted of six CM5Ts; 4801, 4802, 4803, 4804, 4809, 4810 and four CM5s (without toilets and having 37 seats) of which three were soon reconfigured to CM5Ts, 4807 in December 1959, 4805 in January 1960 and 4806 in April 1960. 4808 was left as a CM5 at this stage.

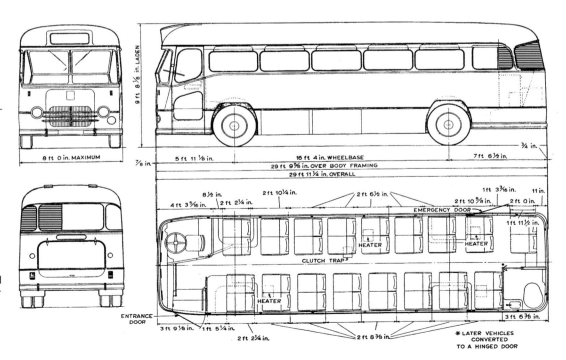

PIONEERS

With the inaugural day approaching, Midland Red had ten[19] motorway coaches ready, these being allocated to Bearwood garage, all having gone through their paces at MIRA and suitably 'run in'. Drivers were carefully selected, being drawn from senior members of the coach driving staff. A team of 17 drivers[20] made up the first selection and were trained in high-speed driving at MIRA. When driving normal buses and coaches in service, drivers had the tendency to change up to a higher gear as soon as possible. When driving the motorway coach they needed to revise their technique. They were instructed to reach near maximum revs in each of the intermediate gears in order to get the best performance from the coach when on the motorway. They were instructed to utilise the middle lane of the motorway as far as possible. This left the fast lane clear for the few cars that could better the coaches' speed, like the Jaguars, whilst leaving the first lane for the commercials and older cars. One cannot help wondering if these drivers were tested for possessing strong bladders, as they were the only ones onboard who could not avail themselves of the toilet at the rear.

Anticipation built up as the big day approached. Nationally, the opening of the M1 Motorway – Britain's first – was attracting attention; and locally, there was added press coverage of the high-speed coach service. The BBC produced a television documentary. This was transmitted at the end of October 1959 and covered the construction and forthcoming opening of the motorway. It included a profile on the Midland Red high-speed coach and the planned new service. Cameras were on board as General Manager, Donald Sinclair, drove a coach around the MIRA track, concluding with an interview. The company's vision was being noticed outside the industry.

On 2nd November 1959, a special commemorative ticket[21] was issued to passengers, which included VIPs and members of the press. At around 8:30 am 4801, which had various 'dignitaries' on board, including Donald Sinclair, and 4803, carrying members of the press, departed from a wet Digbeth Coach Station, amidst firing flashbulbs and much excitement. After all, how many of those passengers had ever had the opportunity to travel by road at around 80 mph before? Most would never have travelled at more than 50 mph, assuming that they had access to a private car.

The route from Digbeth took the A45 Coventry Road – just a few hundred yards from the coach station – and passed through built-up areas until it reached the Birmingham boundary. From here on, it was nearly all dual carriageway until the new motorway network was reached near Dunchurch, where the A45 became the M45. This was a two-lane stretch of motorway, nearly eight miles in length and was the northern spur for the M1. With its flyovers and large blue and white signs and the coaches increasing their speed, some passengers doubtless thought they had reached the M1. The motorways joined at what is now Junction 17 of the M1, about a mile south of the village of Crick. The stretch of M1 travelled by the coaches was 61½ miles. Then near the village of Slip End they joined the southern spur,

Notes

20 C. Attwood, **A. C. Banks**, F. H. Corbett, A. G. Davies, **P. A. H. Daniel**, R. Downing, **H. Fendall**, H. G. Gould, E. Herron, G. Hindle, R. Holliday, **J. G. Miller**, **D. F. Swain**, R. A. Thomas, W. H. Thompson, **F. Tromans** and D. Williams. Those in bold type drove on the first day of operation – 2nd November 1959.

21 The ticket was issued to passengers throughout the month of November 1959.

A commemorative ticket from November 1959.

It's the 2nd November 1959 and the first two Motorway Express coaches head for the M1 Motorway. 4801, with Harry Fendall at the wheel, is carrying dignitaries, whilst 4803 has members of the press on board. T W Moore

the two-lane M10, for the wind down. The M10 was only around three miles long, whereupon the coaches had to contend with London's traffic before reaching Victoria Coach Station.

Jim Pearson, as Development Engineer, was one of those privileged to be on the lead coach and recalls, 'I was fully aware of the coach's capability but even so I was surprised that on the M1 there was no real indication of our actual speed. I particularly remember that as we joined the motorway and started to build up speed, a motorcyclist attempted to overtake us but couldn't and we left him trailing in our wake. It brought home to me what we had achieved.'

The first departure available to the general public was the two o'clock from Digbeth. It left promptly using CM5Ts 4804 and 4809. There was a total of 54 seats taken out of the available 68, leaving room for a TV camera crew (see below). Doubtless there was a novelty element; the oldest passenger was a Mr W. Haynes aged 72, who had witnessed Midland Red's first bus service along the Hagley Road.

As it had not been possible to thoroughly carry out tyre-tests at MIRA and owing to the fact that Midland Red was on the cutting edge of high-speed motorway coach operation, it was considered prudent to have a back-up coach on hand for the first two high-profile vehicles. On board were stowed spare wheels. Bob Richards, who was the driver of this coach on that memorable day says, 'I had a set of spare wheels in the boot, just in case of a problem. Doing the return trip to Birmingham, I was tailing driver Fendall's coach (4801) which had a full load of VIPs. Just on the curve to the join of the M45 spur, the lead coach blew a tyre!'

Jim Pearson who was in the lead coach says, 'Sinclair called me forward to ask what the knocking noise was. We hadn't heard it down the back of the coach but you certainly could at the front! I said that I didn't know. It was in fact a bulge on the tyre. No sooner had I got back to my seat, when the nearside front tyre blew.'

Bob Richards continues, 'I saw Eric Tuff, the Chief Engineer, outside flagging us down. I overshot a few yards and had to reverse up. The passengers and driver transferred to the ghost vehicle from which a spare wheel was provided for the stricken coach. The Dunlop representative was most distraught. Myself and the co-driver replaced the wheel and we arrived at Digbeth twenty minutes behind.' Even after the tyre burst, which was due to a manufacturing fault, the coach was rock steady and was easily brought to a halt on the hard shoulder.

Jim Pearson stayed with 4801 whilst it was jacked up and the work done. 'When I arrived at the party, Sinclair greeted me with something like, "And still you made it within the scheduled time." I think he was trying to make the best of the embarrassment.'

Interestingly, newsreel cameras were filming the events of the day, with film crews at Digbeth and interviews with drivers at Victoria. Aerial shots were taken too and captured driver Fendall's coach, mentioned above, stationary on the hard shoulder. BBC TV had a cameraman on board driver Albert Banks' CM5T, the two o'clock departure from Digbeth. The Motorway Express Service was covered on the evening news and included an interview with Albert Banks. The media were

The inaugural public motorway service was the 2 o'clock departure from Digbeth and involved 4804 and 4809. Ken Jubb

CM5T 4804 was first out of the coach station followed by 4809. Ken Jubb

4809 jockeys for the lead as the two coaches negotiate the traffic on Digbeth High Street. Ken Jubb

Right: **An early view of the M1 Motorway with its central grass reservation. The MOT test had not yet scythed away the pre-war cars.** BMMO

Below: **This cartoon by 'Frostie' appeared in the Midland Red Staff *Bulletin* and depicted four of the first motorway drivers.**

Below right: **The winter of 1959-1960 was far from ideal for an express motorway service. This picture, taken from within CM5T 4805, shows typical weather. Note the Smiths Imperial coach ahead.** Ken Jubb

impressed with his 2 hours 51 minutes journey time.

The first week of operation saw poor weather conditions but the very conservative timings meant only one service arrived late due to dense fog at the London end. Within that first week, the company announced that 63 of the departures between then and Christmas were fully booked and others were substantially booked. The General Manager said, 'We expected a heavy demand in the early stages of the new service because of its novelty value. The indications are that there is a definite public demand apart from the novelty.'

Resplendent in their red and black livery and carrying their somewhat quaint wooden route boards above the side windows, these vehicles were to become familiar sights for the next five or six years. Journeys were comfortable and fast. Journey time between Birmingham Digbeth and London Victoria was initially scheduled at 3 hours 25 minutes, but coaches were consistently arriving around 45 minutes ahead of time. At first, drivers were instructed to try to keep to the scheduled time so as to avoid possible customer inconvenience. A revised time of 2 hours 55 minutes was soon made official. Journey time

The MIDLAND RED

M1

MR. HARRY FENDALL.   MR. DON SWAIN.

COACH DRIVERS by FROSTIE.

MR. PERCY DANIEL.   MR. FRANK TROMANS.

LAND ... SEA ... AND AIR ...

SPEED WITH PERFECT VISION & DRAUGHTLESS VENTILATION

Auster LTD. Established 1841

EQUIPMENT
means reliability
under all
conditions!

Designed to meet the requirements
of modern transport—
Windscreens with shadowless
vision. Easy to operate windows
giving perfect ventilation without
draught and controlled to
individual requirements.
Low maintenance.
Be wise, fit AUSTER.

AUSTER LTD.
BARFORD ST.
BIRMINGHAM 5

NON-STOP **MIDLAND RED** NON-STOP

MOTORWAY EXPRESS
Commencing on Monday, November 2nd, 1959

THE FIRST MOTORWAY EXPRESS IN GREAT BRITAIN

BIRMINGHAM *to* LONDON
DAILY

	a.m.	p.m.	p.m.
BIRMINGHAM (DIGBETH COACH STATION) depart	8.30	2.00	6.30
LONDON (VICTORIA COACH STATION) arrive	11.55	5.25	9.55

LONDON *to* BIRMINGHAM
DAILY

	a.m.	p.m.	p.m.
LONDON (VICTORIA COACH STATION) depart	9.30	1.30	6.30
BIRMINGHAM (DIGBETH COACH STATION) arrive	12.55	4.55	9.55

FARES 13/3 single 21/3 return

ALWAYS IN THE LEAD

The Friendly Midland Red

Printed by Grens & Welburn Ltd., B'ham 7.

Notes

22 In 1961 this was increased to 40 mph and again in 1966 to 50 mph.

spent on the 72 miles of motorways was about one hour, with the remaining time spent getting to and from the motorway, a distance of 44 miles, this being hampered by traffic or the mandatory speed limit for coaches of 30 mph.[22] Later, with urban road improvements, the overall time was modified again, to 2 hours 25 minutes and then to 2 hours 15 minutes.

The service was an unqualified success for Midland Red and passengers alike. The coaches performed magnificently. Over the winter of 1959-1960, only two services arrived

Above left: **Ventilator manufacturer, Auster, was keen to be associated with the prestigious Midland Red motorway coach, as seen in this contemporary advertisement.**

Above: **A Midland Red flyer promoting the new motorway service.**

Left: **CM5T 4807 is seen at Victoria Coach Station on 15th January 1960, having battled its way through dirty weather.**
Mike Greenwood collection

Notes

23 BBC TV History of the Motorways Part One.

24 G. W. Allison, **J. H. Bradshaw**, B. G. Barnes, H. Brown, N. B. Chapman, R. J. Chattaway, B. Ellis, F. W. Izzard, G. Jinks, P. Kenny, D. J. Miller, E. J. Packer, **S. W. Pinfold**, **G. Sparrow**, B. Sharp, **R. G. Taylor, A. W. Walker** and J. E. Wincote. Those in bold type drove on the first day of operation – 1st September 1960.

25 Fleet numbers 4800, 4808 (transferred from Bearwood), 4812 and 4813.

From the beginning, Midland Red's license permitted up to two duplicates. This convoy of three was London-bound. BMMO

late. By 24th July 1960, over 307,000 miles had been covered by the new service and 80,710 passengers carried at a fare of £1 1s 3d (£1.06 approx.) for a return trip. Gross takings reported by BMMO were £39,641 equating to 2s 7d (£0.13 approx.) for every vehicle mile. Average load factor was 29.07 passengers (85.5%). No wonder it was advisable to book in advance! After the initial rush of interest, it might have been expected that loadings would fall off through the winter. This did not prove to be the case. Part of the reason was that the Birmingham New Street-London Euston railway line was undergoing modernisation and services were, as a consequence, being curtailed. Good for Midland Red.

As early as February 1960, the company successfully applied for licences to increase duplication. The thrice daily Birmingham-London-Birmingham service would run with as many as two duplicates. Initially though, only one duplicate was allowed on the evening service out of London. This is likely to have been due to an objection from British Railways. The intention was to space these duplicate departures at intervals of 15 minutes, but coming out of Victoria Coach Station into the busy London streets the coaches could end up in convoy on the motorway. By the following year as many as six coaches for one departure was agreed. A true milestone was reached when, in March 1961, the 16 CM5 and CM5Ts

then in service clocked up one million miles.

When the 1960s dawned, the motorway scene of those days was one viewed with excitement and expectation, mixed with a degree of awe. As commentator Piers Brendon[23] said, 'The M1 was opened in an almost apocalyptic atmosphere. There was a feeling that this road was going to solve Britain's transport problems. There was an enormous excitement about it.' The vast width of the six lanes of motorway plus hard shoulders, divided by a grass reservation; the relatively few vehicles travelling along, many of them pre-war types (the MOT hadn't scythed them away yet); others were more modern saloons, struggling to make 70 mph; then in the outside lane two, even three, of these thoroughly modern-looking coaches running in convoy at 80 mph. Commercial vehicles just didn't do that!

BIRMINGHAM (Digbeth) to LONDON (Victoria)	
depart	*arrive*
8.30 a.m.	11.55 a.m.
2.00 p.m.	5.25 p.m.
6.30 p.m.	9.55 p.m.

LONDON (Victoria) to BIRMINGHAM (Digbeth)	
depart	*arrive*
9.30 a.m.	12.55 p.m.
1.30 p.m.	4.55 p.m.
6.30 p.m.	9.55 p.m.

Coventry Service

Application was also made to introduce a Coventry-London thrice-daily service. A second tranche of drivers[24] numbering 18 was trained to drive the four CM5[25] coaches which arrived at Nuneaton garage, from where the service was to be based. The CM5 was a 37-seat version (no toilet compartment) of the CM5T. The new service commenced on a wet Friday, 1st September 1960. It was given the route number ME2 making the existing Birmingham-London service ME1. In April 1962, the service was extended so that it commenced and terminated at Nuneaton, with an intermediate stop at Bedworth.

COVENTRY (Pool Meadow) to LONDON (Victoria)	
depart	*arrive*
8.30 a.m.	11.00 a.m.
1.00 p.m.	3.30 p.m.
7.00 p.m.	9.30 p.m.

LONDON (Victoria) to COVENTRY (Pool Meadow)	
depart	*arrive*
9.30 a.m.	12.00 p.m.
12.30 p.m.	3.00 p.m.
7.00 p.m.	9.30 p.m.

The Birmingham and Midland Motor Omnibus Co. Ltd.,
Coventry - London Express Service via the New Motorway

INAUGURAL JOURNEY

1st September, 1960

The Friendly Midland Red

The official hand-out, on the inaugural day of the Coventry service, was nothing special. It consisted of a manila cover with a duplicated inside page, on which was mounted a black and white glossy photo.

Seen at Pool Meadow, in the early days of the Coventry-London motorway service, is CM5 4808. Ken Jubb

CM5 4800 was delivered out of sequence in September 1960. It is seen here at Victoria when only a few weeks old. Ken Jubb

Right: **4822 was a C5 that was converted to CM5 standard and arrived at Nuneaton in April 1963. It is seen here at Coventry in September 1963.** Ken Jubb

Below: **Now fitted with twin headlamps, 4808 is seen at Pool Meadow, Coventry in April 1964. Behind is BMMO D9 4931.** Patrick Kingston

Bottom left: **CM5 4800 again, after it had been fitted with twin headlamps. This time it is at Pool Meadow, Coventry, in September 1962.** Ken Jubb

Bottom right: **4837 was the last C5 to be delivered; this was in November 1961. In July 1962, it was converted to CM5 standard and spent some time operating the Nuneaton-Coventry-London service.** R H G Simpson

Worcester Service

Midland Red was ready again on Friday 20th July 1962, when the first section of the M5 Motorway was opened. Five standard C5s (the last ones built) had been taken out of service some months earlier and were converted to CM5s. Three were allocated to Worcester garage and two to Digbeth garage,[26] ready to reduce the existing 1 hour 43 minutes service between Birmingham and Worcester to 50 minutes. This service was given the route number X44 and was faster than the British Rail time! It was in fact a limited stop express and the coaches carried conductors. The service was hourly and on weekdays started from Newport Street, Worcester at 05:55 hours. First run out of Birmingham (Dudley Street) was 06:55 hours. The service utilised 16 miles of the new two-lane M5, from Lydiate Ash near Rubery, at the north end and Whittington, near Worcester, at the southern end. A most pleasant journey, with the Malvern Hills easily visible to the west on all but the cloudiest of days. A typical crew duty would entail four round trips, with a one hour break after the second return trip. It must have been a sought-after job by conductors, there not being that much to do once underway! One may imagine the scene of the conductor standing alongside the driver chatting, as the coach was clocking 75 mph. However, former CM5 driver Basil Twist says, 'I, nor the other motorway coach drivers would have allowed this. Once underway, the conductor remained seated except when taking fares at the two intermediate stops.'

At the end of August, Midland Red was encouraged by passenger numbers. In the first six weeks these totalled 34,667 (17,184 from Birmingham and 17,483 from Worcester).

Notes

26 4833, 4834 and 4835 at Worcester, with 4836 and 4837 at Digbeth.

Top: **This CM5 coach, 4836, was based at Digbeth when the Worcester express service started on 20th July 1962. It is seen here on that date at Digbeth with proud driver Joe Yates.** Andrew Hawthorn collection

Bottom: **After the crash of 4836 in March 1965, 4823 was a replacement for a few weeks. It was photographed at Newport Street, Worcester in April 1965.** Ken Jubb

Below: **The initial Birmingham-Worcester via the Motorway timetable. The illustration on the front cover has been 'fudged'; although it carries route boards along the side and the appropriate wording in the destination box, the photograph used is actually the publicity shot of the first production C5 4774.**

Service No. X44

Motorway Express

Birmingham
(Dudley Street)

Selly Oak
(Oak Tree Lane)

Worcester
(Newport Street)

DAILY SERVICE, NON-STOP
In operation 20th July 1962

'The Friendly Midland Red'

DRIVERS AND PASSENGERS

When these high-speed coaches entered service, drivers were well satisfied with their charges as these were literally a leap forward. In terms of acceleration and speed there had been nothing like it before. Dressed in their white coats and peaked hats the drivers shared the prestige associated with the nation's first motorway and the first express coach service. Even at top speed the coach was very stable, the disc brakes inspired confidence when needing to reduce high speed quickly, the steering was steady and the rubber suspension, being independent at the front, meant that the passengers were not thrown about when the vehicle altered direction.

The large lantern windscreen gave excellent visibility, right down to five and a half feet in front. The driver's seat was of the 'sit up and beg' type, being adjustable forwards and backwards and in height. The long pedal controls were close in to the seat, the driver treading down on them, as they rose almost vertically out of the floor. The large steering wheel was almost horizontal and low-geared (28.5:1), requiring a lot of turning for manoeuvring. The hefty gear lever was to the driver's left coming out of the floor. The handbrake

lever was to the right. In the event of wheel brakes failing, the disc handbrake was considered a good fall-back. Although the gearbox was constant mesh, drivers tended to double declutch both up and down. First gear was only for manoeuvring or getting restarted on hills. Second gear was fine for pulling away, even with a full load. A rule of thumb for maximum gear speeds was, second, 20 mph; third, 40 mph; fourth, 60 mph and fifth, 80 mph. The only instrument provided was a modest speedometer off-set to the left and partly obscured by the steering wheel. This was later joined by a temperature gauge.

During the months following entry into service, professional journalists were permitted to give the CM5T a test drive or at least sample the service. It was John F. Moon of *Commercial Motor* who declared, '... a genuine 75 mph at which speed it was as steady as a rock and as controllable as the most safe of hand-built sports cars.'[27] W.R. Taylor writing in *Passenger Transport* stated: 'The greatest compliment I can pay the CM5 is to tell you that I spend my life road-testing cars, commercial vehicles and public service vehicles and in my years of experience I have tested several cars, even in the upper price range, which are less comfortable, noisier, less pleasant and more difficult to drive than is the CM5.'[28] Later in the same issue of the magazine Robert R. Rodwell said, 'The riding comfort of the CM5 coach at speed was surpassed in quietness and lack of vibration by only one form of transport, jet aircraft.'

Arguably the most readable review was written by D. B. Tubbs and appeared in *Motor.*[29] It commenced, 'The most dramatic way to meet the motorway express is to be passed by it on a wet day. One moment you're ambling up the M1 at 60 mph on the inside lane and the next a nine ton ball of spray hurtles past your right ear at seventy or so. Somewhere, in the middle of the blob, is a great red 34-seat bus, sweeping majestically down the centre lane, as stately as a clipper ship, and as steady as a museum.'

Basil Twist drove one of the Worcester CM5s on the first day the M5 opened. 'I had the shock of my life when I came to get on the motorway at Whittington and saw it was only two lanes! "What's going on here?" I thought. I hadn't realised just what they were building, it wasn't big enough from the word go. We had to watch it with lorries pulling out.

'I'd got into coach work quite quickly. Normally, you had to be with the Midland Red seven or eight years before they'd consider you as a coach driver but I'd done it in five. When our drivers had been chosen for the motorway work, instructors came down from Birmingham with a CM5. We were taken on to the M50 – the Ross Spur – for this. They were very keen

Notes

27 *Commercial Motor* 27th November 1959.

28 *Passenger Transport* 17th August 1960.

29 *Motor* 20th April 1960.

The press, both popular and specialist, were given demonstrations in the CM5T. 4809 was the vehicle used when John Moon (centre) conducted a road test for *Commercial Motor* in November 1959. The driver was probably Ken Worrall, with Jim Pearson also aboard.
Chris Hodge
Trucks Neg no. aax273

to get us confident with using the crawler, or first gear.[30] I don't know why, as we were to do motorway work!

'The CM5 was a beautiful motor. It is true that before they were restricted to 70 mph we would put our foot right down and get whatever we could out of them. Nothing could touch us. I had a blow-out once on the front offside tyre, but it was not a problem making it to the hard shoulder. From there I walked to the yellow emergency phone – no mobile phones then!'

Basil mentions that in recent years he has heard people discussing the pros and cons of the braking system used on BMMO vehicles. He quips, 'I don't recognise the criticisms I sometimes hear. One problem we did have at some stage was the de-misters not working properly. We were issued with demisting gloves!'

BMMO's chosen braking system has come in for criticism, especially when used in stop-start traffic. Indeed unwary drivers who did not use good driving practice could experience difficulty. The CFS braking system on the CM5, saw the servo-assistance pump being belt-driven from the output shaft behind the gearbox. Later the 'beefed-up' DB5/2 gearbox was fitted, and with this the CFS pump was gear-driven from the gearbox. With the CFS system, the degree of assistance provided was proportional to the road speed. This of course was ideal for motorway work, as the faster the vehicle travelled the more powerful the brakes became.[31]

Stan Foxall, another Worcester driver, had been driving C1 coaches on day tours for some years, when the Birmingham–Worcester motorway service began. 'We got three of the CM5 coaches and were told we'd need nine drivers. I was promoted on to that but I do recall having to go for an eye test. We were given a bit of instruction and then a test on the motorway, of course. I guess I was a bit of a speed king, we took them up to whatever we could get out of them. I stayed out of trouble, never had a bump or anything, but I did carry a small spanner and screwdriver! One day I'd come down the M5 in the rain and the nearside wiper was slipping on its spindle. When I came off at Wychbold, I pulled over and fixed

The DB5/2 Gearbox

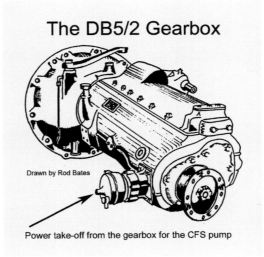

Drawn by Rod Bates

Power take-off from the gearbox for the CFS pump

On the same road test, CM5T 4809 is seen here leaving the M1 slip road at Junction 16 near Weedon.
Chris Hodge
Trucks Neg no. aax274

Notes

30 Changing down from second to first gear was quite demanding, the latter was not constant mesh. Basil recalls driving standard Midland Red coaches and the steep incline at Edgehill on the Banbury road, 'There was a cottage on the left which we used as a marker. You needed to get into first at that point. You had to get it out of second, whip it over the gates, give her a burst on the accelerator and drop it into crawler. If you missed, you needed to be quick on the brake! If you left it until further up the hill and missed your gear, there was a real danger of rolling back.'

31 For a fuller discussion on BMMO's brakes, see *Midland Red's BMMO D9* by Mike Greenwood and Steve Richards especially page 19.

Above: **For a number of years the M1 Motorway could be almost empty of traffic, so Midland Red coaches travelled uninhibited in the first lane, as seen with this Birmingham-bound CM5T.** BMMO

Right: **Birmingham and London non-stop service timetable from 1964.**

Below: **Another delightful cartoon from 'Frostie', which appeared in the staff *Bulletin*.**

Below right: **A CM5T driver talks with passengers while checking tickets.** Transport Museum, Wythall collection

it. You'd be pulled on the carpet for that if they found out. But I always did what was best for my passengers. All in all, I was well satisfied with the CM5 and later the CM6s.'

Initially at least, driver rotas for the London services were on an alternating basis, such that drivers would not be wholly engaged on motorway work. Only one or one and a half round trips in any given duty would be done, the alternate duty being spent on other coach, private hire or even service bus work. The driver and coach of the first day's service from London Victoria would have had an overnight stay in the capital. Driving buses could be more lucrative, as more hours could be worked than on a round motorway duty, especially if the roads were clear. To overcome this, the company introduced 'contract hours', whereby the duty attracted a set time payment rather than actual time worked.

From the passenger's perspective, it should be remembered that in the late 1950s, early 1960s, some people were timid and even fear-ful in respect of the motorway. Add to this the prospect of what was the largest per-missible, fastest-ever coach travelling upon it, and one can see that in some cases there was a barrier to overcome. Popular newspapers in Lon-don and Birmingham and specialist jour-nals worked hard to overcome such res-ervations. As shown earlier by the good load factors, such fears were dispelled.

The wide motor-way, amazing qui-etness and stability of the motorway

Motorway Express

Birmingham
(Digbeth Coach Station)
and
London
(Victoria Coach Station)

DAILY SERVICE, NON-STOP

In operation 26th March, 1964

' The Friendly Midland Red '

CM5Ts 4811 and 4810 head south from Digbeth Coach Station, in August 1962.
BaMMOT

Probably seen in the first year of operation, CM5T 4815 unloads at Victoria Coach Station.
Transport Museum, Wythall collection

The last vehicle to be built as a CM5T from new was 4830. It would be the last of the class to be withdrawn.
Kevin Lane collection

coaches, and, it must be said, the confidence and professionalism of the drivers, actually made the sense of speed less apparent than anticipated.

Passengers were soon expressing their appreciation, being moved to write to Midland Red. Below are extracts taken from two such letters.

'I must write and congratulate you upon the excellent service you have started on the new Motorway. I came to Birmingham especially for the joy of travelling back on your 2 pm journey last Saturday. We left Digbeth on the stroke of the hour, and IT WAS THE MOST ENJOYABLE AND COMFORTABLE JOURNEY I HAVE YET UNDERTAKEN BY ANY MEANS OF TRAVEL – and I am now in my early fifties … I shall treasure my special ticket, and look forward to my next journey.'

'Having recently completed the double journey to London in one of your new Express Coaches on the Motorway, I would like to say how much my wife and I enjoyed the experience. The organisation was beyond criticism and we travelled in absolute comfort each way.

'I would like to pay a high tribute to the driver – it so happened we had the same one each time and his care and skill both on the road itself and in the London traffic was good to behold. Our congratulations to you, and best wishes for the future.'

For the first time, people could visit the Capital for a useful time span – about six hours – returning the same day, at a fraction of the rail fare. Not only was this appealing to those visiting for leisure but also to those within the business community. Nor was it all one way traffic. In the first nine months 44.65% of passengers started from London.

BMMO CM5T SPECIFICATION

ENGINE
Type S14 KL turbocharged.
Horizontal 6 cylinder in-line diesel, direct injection.
Bore   4.450 in.
Stroke   5.250 in.
Capacity 8.028 litres.
CAV exhaust turbocharger fitted.
138 bhp at 1,900 rpm.
Maximum torque 430 lb/ft at 1,400 rpm.

CLUTCH
Single dry-plate, 15⅞ in. diameter.

GEARBOX
BMMO DB5 constant-mesh gearbox.
Gear ratios:
   First   4.968:1
   Second   2.74:1
   Third   1.617:1
   Fourth   1:1 (direct)
   Fifth   0.73:1 (overdrive)
   Reverse   6.429:1

REAR AXLE
Fully floating unit with Kirkstall hypoid-bevel drive.
Ratio 4.44:1.

BRAKES
BMMO-Girling disc brakes with Lockheed continuous-flow-powered hydraulic system, giving 4:1 servo effect, operating on front and rear wheels. Mechanically operated transmission handbrake, 16 in. diameter disc type, with cable-operated bi-sector unit.

SUSPENSION
Metalastik variable-rate rubber suspension front and rear. Inclined bonded sandwich units at front, and double torsional toggle links at rear. Independent front suspension, trailing arm and upper wishbone system. Rear suspension adjustable for height. Armstrong telescopic dampers at all wheels.

STEERING
Marles double-cam steering box. Ratio 28.5:1.

TURNING CIRCLES
62ft both locks; swept* circles, 68ft 6 in. both locks.
(* this takes into account the body overhang)

TYRES
Front 10.00x20 in. 14 ply; rear 9.00x20 in. 10 ply.

FUEL TANK
35-gallon capacity.

ELECTRICAL
24-volt starting and lighting equipment, four 6-volt 135-amp-hr batteries.

FRAME
All steel welded construction integral with body.

BODY ITEMS

Dimensions	Overall length	29ft 9⅝ in.
	Overall width	8ft 0 in.
	Front overhang	5ft 11⅛ in.
	Wheel base	16ft 4 in.
	Rear overhang	7ft 6½ in.
Windows	12 side windows above which Auster hopper-type ventilators. Lantern type windscreen.	
Heating	Three Clayton Dewandre recirculatory units. Demisters fitted to front screens.	
Ventilation	Fan-assisted ventilation fitted in the front bulkhead, together with an extractor fan to the rear canopy.	
Seats	34 coachbuilt seats with adjustable headrests.	
Toilet	Compartment at rear nearside. Chemical type.	
Unladen weight	6 tons 18 cwt. Distribution 3 tons 6 cwt on front wheels, 3 tons 12 cwt on rear wheels.	

MAINTENANCE AND MODS

High-speed coach operation was uncharted territory and BMMO was well aware that the development of the motorway coach, which had started in earnest less than eight months before the operation began on 2nd November 1959, meant that the work was not over. Testing continued and monitoring of components would need to be in-hand to see how they stood up to this service use. As with motoring today, town work and motorway work is a matter of swings and roundabouts as far as wear and tear is concerned. For the CM5, there was less clutch use and gear changing than for the average service buses of that time. Likewise the brakes would have been used less often but when they were, it was more heavy usage.

General maintenance was straightforward and made no special demands on staff over that normally expended on other vehicles in the fleet. The engine, gearbox, propeller shaft, brakes and hypoid bevel rear end, each of which required regular attention, were easily accessible for pit servicing. There were 26 lubrication nipples. Of these 3 were on the propeller shaft, 12 on the steering linkage and king pins and the others were split into two groups, serving pedal controls at the front and the engine control linkage at the rear. The rubber suspension units reduced the amount of maintenance time. Disc brakes were much easier to maintain; changing friction pads on a complete vehicle was timed at one man-hour, compared with eight for linings on drum brakes. Other work, like cleaning of air filters, could be done by lifting hinged fibreglass panels located below the waist line.

From the start, a daily pit inspection was performed on each coach at its home garage. Nothing untoward was manifest. After a year of operation, each vehicle had done an average of 80,000 miles and was subjected to a special inspection at the Central Works. In addition, a few major running-units were removed and dismantled, so that a detailed examination could be made. All of this was as an insurance against the unexpected but also as a means of gathering data to assess what wear and tear could be anticipated.

With motorway express services underway Jim Pearson says, 'I was becoming concerned about some of the reports from drivers regarding the high speeds they were reaching. I was worried about the demands this would be placing on the tyres. I got the engine speed governed down accordingly.' It was decided that the available 80+ mph could be reduced to 75 mph. Earlier, the engine speed had been upped to a governed 2,200 rpm; it was now reduced to 1,950 rpm without loss of power. This was possible partly because a revised form of fuel delivery valve was used and a spring link was fitted between the governor and the fuel pump rack to give a more definite governor cut-off. This allowed maximum power, right up to the governor's cut-off point, by means of limit stops in the fuel pump. The fuel pumps were also recalibrated.[32] This done, the coaches averaged a fuel consumption of slightly over 14 mpg. With scheduled times already being accomplished with ease, this modification had no detrimental effect on the service offered.

As a result of service experience, it was found necessary to introduce adjustable radiator shutters and a water temperature gauge was also fitted. The shutters were located between the grille and the radiator and were controlled by the driver. Later a more sophisticated design of radiator shutter was fitted, automatically operated by a wax-filled capsule placed in the engine cooling water system. The

Notes

32 At first this was 22cc per 200 shots and altered to 19cc per 200 shots at 300rpm.

C5 4795 is being refuelled. Fuel consumption for the turbocharged versions was particularly good, averaging 14.1 mpg.
A T Willis

33 Air pressure was 85 psi on the front and 45 psi for each of the four rear tyres.

34 A few motorway coaches had a stacked lamp arrangement, which would later appear on the CM6 class. However, the arrangement did not last long on the CM5 class and was replaced by the side by side unit.

Below: **Fuel consumption graph for the BMMO CM5.**

Below right: **After a few years of motorway use, oil thrown out from the engine was a problem. Shields were fitted to protect the rear offside forward suspension unit and the disc handbrake.**

automatic shutters were introduced on the Worcester CM5s. Radiator shutters ensured that the water temperature could be maintained at a level for the most efficient running of the engine and, it was said, to obtain a satisfactory temperature within the saloon, complementing the three Clayton Dewandre heaters located beneath the seats.

Turbocharger, clutch, gearbox and differential were showing little in the way of wear. Steering mechanisms also showed no more than normal wear.

Ingress of foreign objects, thrown up by fast turning wheels on the motorway, was causing some concern. Exposed components located on the underside were vulnerable as well as brakes. Although the disc brakes as a whole were causing no problems, brake pad life was reduced, due more to entry of abrasives than actual use. This necessitated brake pad changes at about 35,000 miles instead of the 45,000-50,000 on stage-carriage services. Abrasive material was also getting into the lubricants and more adequate sealing was necessary.

High engine speeds, when combined with wear and tear on engine components, would result in leaking oil being thrown back towards the rear offside. This was particularly harmful to the offside forward rubber suspension unit. Shields were fitted to protect these parts and the disc handbrake.

The tyres continued to be an issue. Within the first two years some 15 makes and types were evaluated. The first motorway coaches used rayon cord 9.00x20 in. (12 ply front and 10 ply rear).[33] This was soon changed to nylon cord 10.00x20 in. 14 ply being fitted on the front and 9.00x20 in. 10 ply on the rear. These were Dunlop Highway tyres which had a shallower tread than other commercial vehicle tyres, this having the effect of more readily dissipating heat associated with high-speed travel. After two years of operation and 1.5 million miles no tyre had failed other than through normal punctures. Dunlop, Michelin and Firestone each ended up with a share in the market to

provide Midland Red with its specific requirements. As testing on the motorway proved, tyres of a steel radial ply construction were the coolest running tyre. Eventually all tyre companies adopted this form of construction pioneered by Michelin.

The new M1 Motorway came in for criticism in regard to the high amount of surface water during wet weather. As with the ingress of debris, this showed up insufficient attention to sealing. Components like electrical junction boxes were vulnerable as were the generators for the electric speedometer. The latter was resolved by placing them in polythene bags.

Another problem cited here as a final anecdote from engineer Bob Richards was the mystery of wet suitcases in the boot. To ascertain the cause, Bob was made comfortable in the boot and taken for a ride down the motorway at high-speed, '…on a wet day of course! It was no big deal really. I had a little 24 volt light to see by and although I can't remember for certain, we probably just did a run up the M45. It soon became apparent that the holes drilled in the boot's floor to drain water were actually allowing it in. The air pressure beneath the vehicle was such that, at speed, it forced a fountain of water through the holes. The solution was to install a fan in the boot, beneath the toilet compartment.' At first it was assumed that the boot door needed additional sealing to combat water being driven in by vortices. Once the true cause was confirmed, the centrifugal fan not only assisted in moving air from the toilet compartment, but increased air pressure in the luggage area, so stopping air and water entering the luggage area.

One of the easiest modifications to spot was the contemporary inclination towards twin headlamps. This was no mere fashion trend for BMMO. The new lamp arrangement enabled one pair to be adjusted for dipped and the other for main beam. Within each headlamp set, the two lamps could be individually angled, which improved the projection of the dipped beam over that obtained

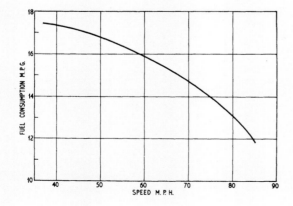

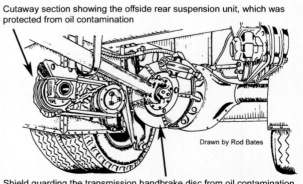

Cutaway section showing the offside rear suspension unit, which was protected from oil contamination

Drawn by Rod Bates

Shield guarding the transmission handbrake disc from oil contamination

A small number of CM5Ts were given additional headlamps, together with a second fog light, fitted as seen here. These were soon superseded by the side-by-side layout. Nevertheless, the vertical arrangement reappeared on the CM6 class. R H G Simpson

when using a single double filament bulb.[34]

A further modification, which was also outwardly visible, was the raising of the front bumper. As early as 1961, some coaches across the C5 class had the bumper raised by two inches. This spoiled the appearance of the front end a little, as the passenger step was exposed beneath the bumper and the radiator grille now appeared to sit on top of the bumper. Obviously, ground clearance must have been a problem which could not be addressed by the limited adjustment available in the suspension set up.

Despite the design attention to ventilation, passenger discomfort was evident during hot weather. To help ease this problem, by late 1960 some coaches began to appear with a broad white panel painted on the roof to reflect heat. This was done with care, so that it was only visible from above and did not detract from the red and black livery. Both Jim Pearson and Bob Richards recall experimenting with two biscuit tin lids, painting one black and the other white. A hole was drilled in each and a cork inserted to hold a thermometer. The solar heat absorption on the black one proved beyond doubt the

After the motorway coaches had done their first year's service, they were given a thorough check-over. The opportunity was taken to fit twin headlamps and an additional fog light, as seen here on 4833, photographed at Newport Street, Worcester, in April 1965. Ken Jubb

CM5T 4826 is awaiting delivery to Bearwood garage in March 1961. It was built with twin headlamps from new. BMMO

Many of the C5 class had their front bumper raised for improved ground clearance. Here, 4787 is seen before and after the modification. R Norton and R H G Simpson

value of painting the roof white. In 1963, most coaches had two opening roof lights fitted. 4809 was given experimental electrically operated roof lights. These would reappear on the later CM6T class. In May 1962, 4830 was fitted with the Smiths forced air ventilation system, soon to be used on the S17 and CM6 class. This gave the passenger individual ventilation control through their own air jet nozzle, which was located beneath the parcel rack.

Following on from ventilation, this is a good place to mention that in 1960, 4801, followed by some other motorway coaches (e.g. 4804 and 4806), had cigarette machines installed at the rear of the saloon.

The lantern windscreen was initially of toughened glass; this was changed for laminated glass. Drivers requested better mirrors and soon larger wing mirrors were put in place. An additional rear view mirror was provided.

Over the period that the C5 class was built (1958-1961), there were numerous subtle differences, innovations and one-offs. A few, not mentioned elsewhere in the main text, include: on early examples the inspection panel on the offside was removable, held in place by four locks at each corner, but this design was superseded by a top hinged panel; after the first half dozen or so built, the rear side window was modified to give a more raked appearance; at one stage 4788 had a sliding window in the passenger door; later coaches had two outward opening doors (with associated stops) for the boot, instead of the single upward-opening door; a simple aperture in the front panel housed the fog lamp on early coaches, but soon this aperture was contoured to encompass it; the profile of the rear roof ventilator, which at first had been similar to that of the S14, was altered in 1959; polished mouldings varied on the grille, in particular the central vertical piece. Moving to the interior: the earlier step light was circular, later square; early headrests were in the floral moquette but later a buff leather was used; 4784 was used to try out the leopard-skin moquette later to be a feature of the motorway coaches; 4774 had newspaper nets on the back of the seats, the Worcester CM5s had a fold down table on the seat backs; 4774, and possibly some of the other early coaches, had window openers like those on the S15, but the standard C5 opener was a black knob which was rotated; there was some variation to colour scheme for the instrument panel but most were buff with a red top; 4796 had fluorescent lighting and bulkhead fans had simplified controls on later coaches.

After a couple of years of Nuneaton garage being involved with the motorway coaches, all but the most basic maintenance was transferred to the Midland Red Area Dock at Wigston. In addition to being a garage, Wigston had comprehensive workshops. These provided a full back-up for other Midland Red garages in the Leicester area. A body shop, plastics shop (fibreglass), trim shop and engineering pits were all available. Nuneaton's motorway coaches were serviced each week at Wigston and heavier work, which otherwise would have been done at Central Works, was also carried out here.

When these coaches arrived at Wigston for more careful attention, they were the immediate responsibility of garage hand, Peter O'Sullivan, with trainee assistant, Rod Bates. After a year Peter moved and Rod, who wasn't quite 18 years of age, along with a 15 year-old to assist, continued the work under foreman Les Ayres.

Rod, who had studied all of the technical literature on the motorway coach even before Wigston's involvement, was extremely conscientious and with the aid of personal notes recalls: 'We had nine of the motorway coaches, fleet numbers 4779 [a CS5, see later], 4800, 4808, 4812, 4813, 4822, 4831, 4832, and 4837.

'The plan was that we would be given one vehicle per day for four days a week to service and the CS5 was to come to us once a month for inspection.

'When we first got them, an inspection of the fleet revealed a number of faults. Defects, some of which were common to all, included: Greasy front wheels; slack timing chains; wide tappet clearances; noisy shock absorbers; uneven clutch adjustment; oil throw out; the flexible brake hoses were maladjusted on four of the vehicles; partially seized hand brake callipers on two of them, probably due to salt and road dirt ingress, and finally, on one coach, the rear suspension unit was shearing from its bonding, this most likely as a result of oil contamination.'

The performance of individual coaches would vary. Rod singles out 4813 and 4832 as being particularly fast. He says that when assistant foreman Ray Morris came to Wigston to take up his post, he was most impressed when shown over the CM5 by Rod. Until this time Les had done the test drives after servicing but Ray was keen to have a go. Rod, who was usually present on these trips says, 'Ray was complimentary about the coach and I felt very proud. I remember him throwing the coach into a corner at 70 mph on our way back from Arnesby. "They stick to the road like glue." he said. Les, who was much older, swore and told him to slow down! On another occasion Ray took us over to Northampton and then back on the motorway. Again Les told him to slow down from 70 mph as we were running the engine in! Policy at that time was that they were half run-in on the test bed at Central Works and then fitted to the vehicle to complete the running-in.'

PROMOTIONS AND DEMOTIONS

Notes

35 Standard C5 coaches were receiving the five-speed gearboxes as these became available.

36 4774, 4779, 4785, 4794 and 4795. Note 4779 was promoted once again in early 1963 when it became a CM5.

37 4777, 4784, 4786 and 4796. Note 4777 actually became a CM5 at this point and then a CS5 later in the year.

38 4801, 4802, 4805, 4806, 4811, 4822, 4823, 4826 and 4837.

39 4806 and 4811 retained their toilets even though downgraded to CS5.

In order to provide more flexibility within the fleet, some vehicles in the standard C5 class were upgraded. The purpose for this was that whilst the coaches retained a primary coaching role they could, when required, also be used for motorway work. The fuel injector pressure was increased, suspension is likely to have been stiffened and front-tyre size presumably increased to the 10.00x20 in. size. A 5-speed overdrive gearbox was fitted if not already.[35] This class was designated CS5 and would have been capable of 65 mph. The CS5s were useful for providing duplicates on the motorway services. Whilst lacking the acceleration, top speed and presumably fuel efficiency of their turbocharged brethren, they were obviously considered a success. Nine coaches which had started life as standard C5s were upgraded in two batches. At the end of 1961, five[36] were modified and a further four[37] in Spring 1963. Between early 1965 and March 1966, nine[38] of the turbocharged vehicles, which had done their time on dedicated motorway work, were downgraded to CS5 specification, losing their toilets[39] where fitted and reverting to 37-seat layout. It is likely that this batch of coaches

would have been re-engined while retaining their higher-speed rear axle. This being so, theoretically at least, they would have had the edge in terms of speed over the earlier CS5s when employed on motorway work.

Whenever non-toilet vehicles were used on the Birmingham–London service, drivers were obliged to offer the passengers a toilet stop. Interestingly, though the onboard toilet was used frequently, when a toilet was not available, passengers tended to restrain themselves rather than ask the driver to turn into the motorway services!

Tim Brown, who later became a Midland Red bus driver, recalls travelling on a CS5. 'I was a passenger on a summertime day excursion from Birmingham to Blackpool which had been doing 70 mph or thereabouts for about an hour on the M6. As we pulled onto the slip-road for a service station break, there was a *whoosh* sound and a cloud of steam billowed up on the outside and inside of the windscreen, just above the radiator. On being asked what caused this, the driver said something to the effect: "These coaches very often do it when the power comes off after a long, fast motorway stretch. So no need to worry."'

Tim observes, 'Buses and coaches built by BMMO were equipped with a speedo and had no other gauges to check oil pressure or water temperature, so there was no way of knowing what was happening amidships unless nasty mechanical noises dominated the engine noise, by when it was usually too late. For some reason, Central Works engineers never fitted a fan behind the radiator of their single-deckers.'

Jim Pearson confirms the omission of a fan on the underfloor engined vehicles, but points out that no problems of this nature occurred with the CM5. Indeed, the matter never became acute enough for BMMO engineers to consider the introduction of a cooling fan. However, as coaches got older, and perhaps maintenance played a part, then clogged grilles and sediment in the radiator could result in 'pocketed steam'. When an engine, which had been working hard, came to rest, an inefficient radiator could allow a heat build-up and if there was excessive heat in one or more of the cylinder heads, this would turn the water into steam, which would escape wherever it could. Some work was done in order to avoid problems i.e. the repositioning of the engine thermostat so as to be more responsive to engine outlet water temperatures; the widening of the water passages between the cylinder block and cylinder heads to improve water flow and, as mentioned already, radiator shutters (when fitted) were made automatic, so that their correct usage was not reliant upon the driver.

Between 1965-1969 45 C5s of all variants were demoted to bus work, these being desig-

Opposite page:

The first production CM5T was downgraded to CS5 standard in March 1965. The most obvious external clues are the removal of the toilet compartment and route boards above the side windows. The destination, Cheltenham, also points to this downgrading. Transport Museum, Wythall collection

4823 was one of a number which started life as a standard C5, and was then promoted to CM5, demoted to CS5 and finally demoted once again to C5A standard. It was photographed here when designated a CS5. Travel Lens Photographic

This page:

Making the more sedate journey to London, via Aylesbury, is CS5 4784. This fine photograph was taken on the A34 Stratford Road in Hall Green, Birmingham, in June 1969. Malcolm Keeley

The C5A bus had a power-operated door which necessitated the removal of a section of the wrap-around bumper. BMMO

This view of 4779 highlights the C5A door. The picture is interesting because the vehicle retains its coach livery and is seen in London. R H G Simpson

This page:

This Southgate Street, Leicester-based C5A 4804 is operating the 664 route and is seen in Oxford Street, Leicester. Behind is a Daimler DD13 Fleetline. Photobus

Being based at Worcester, C5A 4817 had plenty of rural work. J E Tennent

Seen at Leamington Spa bus station in May 1970 is C5A 4807. Behind is S22 fleet number 5892. Patrick Kingston

Opposite page:

Working route L43, a Leamington Spa town service, in March 1971 is C5A 4826. T W Moore

C5A 4794 spent one month working out of Cradley Heath garage. It is seen here in Graingers Lane, Cradley Heath at the beginning of May 1971. Paul Gray

nated C5A. The door was converted to power operation and opened inward, necessitating the removal of the nearside short section of front bumper. The new door had an increased glazed area. However, one example, 4778, had a 'jack-knife' centre-folding door. A driver's compartment was installed, a stanchion being fitted either side of the start of the gangway, with a perspex bulkhead attached, one behind the driver and the other separating the front nearside seat from the entrance steps. The destination box was altered to accommodate a small digit three-track blind, below which was a destination blind. A used ticket box and waybill holder were put in place. Existing seat moquette was retained, and where a toilet was fitted, this was removed and in its place three seats were installed with appropriately patterned moquette. Of course, if the vehicle had a turbocharger fitted, it was removed. The rear curved perspex windows were either painted white, black or left clear. In most cases, starting with 4806 in 1970, one-man-operation equipment was provided. As a C5A could have originated from any one of the four previous variants (C5, CM5, CM5T and CS5), differences were legion, which may have been compounded by garages swapping components from vehicle to vehicle.

It was not an ideal vehicle for bus work and was often given little more than local town workings. Conductors found that the aisle proved quite awkward. This complaint

is documented in formal minutes[40] relating to discussions between the local trade union and management at Evesham garage. The management sympathised and agreed that the type would be restricted to routes with light loadings. The same minutes also record the question of whether these vehicles should be viewed as coaches when used on private hire or long distance services. This mattered because coach drivers were of a more exalted rank than were bus drivers. Just because the type was now being driven by the latter, it was a delicate issue as to how far the privilege should be extended! The answer was returned some months later;[41] no bus drivers to be used on private hire or long distance work.

Notes

40 Minutes dated 9th December 1966.

41 In a letter from the management dated 18th June 1967. One wonders what arrangement was in place during the intervening six months.

ACCIDENTS

On the evening of Friday 25th November 1960, CM5T 4809 departed from Digbeth on the 6.30 pm service to London. At the wheel was driver Frank Tromans; he had a full load on board. Near disaster struck ninety minutes later when the coach was two miles north of the Newport Pagnell services. It was travelling in the fast lane at between 65-70 mph and it would appear that conditions were wet.

David Swinfen, a 23-year-old post-graduate student at Birmingham University, was a passenger on board. He describes what happened, 'A large black car was in the centre lane in front of us. It came out into the fast lane in front of our coach. Our driver pulled over, touched the grass central reservation, and, before we had time to think, we were in a jumble of bodies and luggage. There was no panic. Someone opened the emergency door at the back, but most of us stayed in the bus until the police came, because it was very wet outside.'

The coach had slewed round 180 degrees as it struck the central reservation, which at that time was no more than mud and grass. It toppled onto its nearside, facing the oncoming traffic. Amazingly, only three passengers were slightly injured. One passenger was taken to hospital suffering from shock. Subsequently, the passengers were transported to Newport Pagnall services and then onto Victoria by a replacement coach arriving at 25 minutes after midnight, two and a half hours late!

Initially, the coach was moved to a garage at Old Stratford near Milton Keynes before being taken back to Central Works, Edgbaston. After repair it reappeared with stacked twin headlamps, although these would be replaced later with the more familiar side-by-side twin headlamp arrangement. The coach then resumed motorway services from its home at Bearwood garage.

Friday 19th March 1965 saw CM5 4836 set out from Worcester for Birmingham on the second service of the day (06:55 hrs). Eddie Finch was the driver, Jack Willis the conductor and there were eight passengers on board. The CM5 had only been travelling on the M5 for less than ten minutes and was cruising at 65 mph when a car, joining the motorway at Junc-

Swerving at 60 m.p.h to avoid a car, this is what happened to a Birmingham-London Midland "Red" high-speed motor coach when it overturned on the "fast" lane of the M.1 motorway near Newport Pagnell, Buckinghamshire, last night. It was badly damaged, but none of its 34 passengers was seriously hurt.

tion 5, caused the coach to swerve and skid on the greasy surface of the motorway, crossing the central reservation and the south bound carriageways, fortunately not colliding with any oncoming traffic. It careered through the safety fence, down a 20ft embankment, turning onto its roof in the process. It came to rest at a fence separating the embankment from the garden of a bungalow, blocking a side road.

One of the passengers, Richard Norman, who was a sports sub-editor with the *Evening Mail and Despatch*, explained, 'We had not been on the motorway long, and had just reached the junction for Droitwich. The road was very greasy. Suddenly the bus went into a front wheel skid and careered across the road... rolled over and down the bank... We had to scramble through the smashed windows... there was a strong smell of fumes and we were afraid the bus might catch fire any minute. The smashed windows gave us a quick way out.'

It was a terrifying ordeal for all on board. As with the incident involving 4809, it is amazing that the injuries were relatively minor. Fire and ambulance services were soon on the scene and all ten people were taken to Bromsgrove Cottage Hospital. Cuts and bruises, the former the result of flying glass, were the main injuries but there was one who had a broken rib and another a broken arm. However, all were discharged the same day.

On the day of the crash, Midland Red management trainee John Morris was on 'work experience' at Bearwood. On that day he was

This page:

Two dramatic pictures of CM5 4836, as they appeared in the *Worcester News*.

Testimony to the structural integrity of the body, 4836 was back in service in June 1966. However, it was rebuilt as a C5A bus and allocated to Malvern garage, where it is seen here. Christopher Davis

Opposite page:

A newspaper cutting showing a night time picture of CM5T 4809 on its side.

The damaged 4809 seen the following day at Central Works.
Photo via Andrew Hawthorn

Photographed on 12th June 1967 at Central Works, two days after its major accident, is C5A 4812. It was never rebuilt and so was sold for scrap in February 1968. BMMO

C5 4789 spent the first half of the 1960s on coaching duties from Southgate Street, Leicester. It was on a trip to Weymouth, travelling along the A36 at Limpley Stoke, when it had an altercation with a Vauxhall Cresta and a signpost.
Photo via Martin Hobson

in the office of L.H. Youngs, the Staff Manager. Over 45 years later he recalls what must have been exciting stuff for a 17-year-old.

'The 'phone rang and I answered it. It turned out that all major accidents had to be reported to this office and the call was to advise that a motorway express coach, on route to Birmingham from Worcester, had lost control, crossed the central reservation, hurtled across the opposite carriageway, missing the oncoming traffic, and then dived nose first down the bank on the other side. It then cartwheeled over to land on its roof.

'The "White Elephant" breakdown truck was duly called out to recover the vehicle. The procedure at that time was that any seriously damaged vehicle was wrapped in tarpaulin, before being towed through the city, so as to avoid any negative publicity for the company.'

At the time of the crash 4836 had been on loan to Worcester garage from Digbeth. It had extensive repair to the body work carried out at Central Works before going into store and was converted to a C5A bus in May of the following year.

A third serious accident involved 4812 after it had been demoted from CM5 to a C5A. On Saturday 10th June 1967, the vehicle was used on the Associated Motorways Leicester-Barry Island, South Wales service.[42] The vehicle and driver, Roy Freer, were based at Wigston garage.

The coach departed from Digbeth Coach Station at 08:30 hrs. At 11:45 hrs, whilst on the A449 Usk-to-Caerleon road, the bus allegedly suffered a front nearside tyre burst.[43] It ploughed through a hedgerow and struck a tree before coming to a halt. Such was the impact that the front and offside were wrecked.

There was no panic but the driver was trapped and, to add to the confusion, the engine continued to race due to throttle damage. A passing motorist raised the alarm. Thirteen people were taken to the Gwent Hospital. Injuries were mainly lacerations and shock, although a 12-year-old boy sitting behind the driver received a fractured skull. Driver, Roy Freer, was more seriously hurt but eventually recovered and returned to work.

4812 was back at Central Works two days later but never repaired. It was sold to a scrap dealer the following February.

OUT OF SERVICE

Withdrawals of all C5 classes were, for the main part, condensed into a one year period commencing in October 1970. 4812 had been withdrawn in January 1968 following an accident, and the first production C5, 4774, was taken out in February 1970, having been on bus work at Oldbury garage. The last C5A, 4817, finished at Malvern in November 1971; 4799 and 4824, both standard C5 coaches, retired at Shrewsbury garage the following month. On paper at least, the final withdrawal was CM5T 4830, which was withdrawn in July 1972 but had been in store since the previous September. This coach had maintained its original configuration being used as the company directors' coach. Mike Holloway was a CM6T driver at Digbeth in the early 1970s and recalls how 4830 was a useful vehicle to have to hand. 'I drove it a number of times as a duplicate down to London, when things were busy. It was good to drive it, knowing it was something of a veteran. In fact, I drove it on its last revenue-earning trip. The Omnibus Society hired it for an outing to Southend Transport in 1971.' Mike's own view was, 'It was tail-heavy and could catch you out with a slide in wet conditions.'

Midland Red vehicles were never popular on the second-hand market. There was the perception that spares would be hard to obtain, though in reality many were products of outside component manufacturers. Nevertheless, it is true that there were always easier options on the market.

In all 16 of the C5 class were sold on.[44] Four vehicles 4785, 4816, 4827 and 4836, went to Margo International Coachlines of London. 4794 sailed to Eire and 4830 to the USA, the latter, like 4780, being used as a mobile home. Hulleys of Baslow took on 4795 but it lasted less than two years with them. It re-emerged as a stockcar transporter. 4819 fared much better, becoming the Lichfield Speedway Supporters Club coach and benefited from the care given to it by some supporters who were also Midland Red employees. After the club had finished with it, 4819 moved into preservation and remains to this day. It is currently owned by Dave Parry and is resident at the Wythall Transport Museum in Worcestershire. 4780 mentioned above was rescued for restoration by Andrew Hawthorn in 1998 but the task was too great and so Roger Burdett took over the work in 2004. After tremendous work and no little expense the vehicle was back on the road in 2009, looking magnificent.

Notes

42 A summer Saturdays only service, routing via Coventry-Birmingham-Cheltenham-Cardiff.

43 It was subsequently proved in court, that the tyre had not burst prior to the vehicle leaving the road.

44 For more on all withdrawals and further use see Appendix H.

CM5T 4830 was the last of that variant to be built and remained in service the longest. It was still being used from Digbeth in 1971.
Ken Jubb

Top: **Two of the C5 class went overseas. 4830 to the USA, and 4794 to Eire. The latter is seen here looking forlorn in the mid-1970s. Its Irish registration was 5275 ZJ.** Ken Jubb

Above: **Hulleys of Baslow acquired CS5 4795 in 1971, but its time there was short-lived. The coach to the left is KBN 90, an AEC Reliance with Burlingham body, and the one to the right, the very rare Guy Warrior with Plaxton body, registration JBV 234.** Ken Jubb

Above right: **After leaving Hulleys, 4795 became a stock car transporter. It is seen here along with 4809, both vehicles being owned by a Mr Day of Warley, West Midlands. The intention was that 4795 would provide spares for his restoration of 4809. Sadly, both were ultimately scrapped.** Ken Jubb

Right: **Probably the most famous of the surviving C5s is 4819, which was seen for many years in its striking yellow and black livery, the colours of Lichfield Speedway.** Andrew Hawthorn Collection

PART TWO

Maintaining
the Momentum

The BMMO CM6T, CM6 and CM6A

Seen when new, CM6T 5652 London-bound
on the A45 in 1965. T W Moore

NEW MODEL

As a bus manufacturer, Midland Red had been lobbying the Ministry of Transport for a relaxation of the dimensions permitted for buses, which since 1950 had kept single-deckers at 30ft long by 8ft wide. So keen was the company to present its case, that it went to great lengths (!) to do so. In early 1959, a start was made on a mock-up vehicle based on an S8 service bus 3220 (JHA 820). It was built to the fantastic length of 45ft. Having secured a special dispensation, it was driven to London on three occasions (probably all in the first half of 1960). On board were representatives of the Metropolitan Police, Ministry of Transport and Midland Red. It is assumed that, as the idea was to float the plausibility of a 60-seat (plus toilet) motorway coach, these journeys to Victoria Coach Station were made using the motorway. What effect this effort had is not recorded but, on 1st August 1961, the Construction and Use Regulations were adjusted to permit bus dimensions of 36ft long by 8ft 2½ in wide. These were known as the new 'box' dimensions.

In the late 1950s, in anticipation of the revised regulation, the Design Office of BMMO had started preliminary work for the increase in length of the S14/S15/C5 range of vehicles, with the emphasis on stage carriage models. The fruit of this work was the S16 and S17 single-deck buses.

It was not until the middle of 1961 that a 36ft coach design was produced and discussions held with Metal Sections Ltd. The design provided for a 46-seater, plus a toilet. The power unit would be a BMMO 10.5 litre horizontal engine, with a standard five-speed overdrive gearbox. The brakes were as with the CM5, although the Lockheed tandem accumulator system was to be used. This was on account of the heavier weights involved and would give more immediate assistance at low engine

revs. Suspension was again as with the CM5, except that the rear suspension units would be of the heavier specification, as used on the D9 double-deck bus.

For the passengers there were to be individual forced-air jet nozzles. Those in the Traffic Department were disappointed with the design, as they were expecting to accommodate 46 large suitcases in the boot.

In August 1962, the prototype CM6T 5295 (5495 HA) was handed over to the Development Engineer, Jim Pearson, and his team at the Development Department. The first priorities were to weigh the coach in both unladen and laden conditions and to arrange a tilt test. This was successfully completed in early September. A series of tests were carried out at MIRA, on the M1 and restarts on local steep gradients. The braking deceleration and fade tests undertaken at MIRA were satisfactory.

By the end of 1962, 4,500 miles had been covered, including general running-in and high speed tyre tests. These tests were carried out on the M1 Motorway in conjunction with Dunlop and Firestone. Both of these suppliers confirmed that they were satisfied with the 10.00x20 tyre size on the front wheels. Tests on ride quality were undertaken and, as a result, the shock absorber settings were modified for both front and rear dampers. Finally, as this development work was undertaken in the winter period, the decision was taken to test a Varivane automatic radiator shutter.

Outwardly, the prototype CM6T looked at first and second glance like a CM5T but 6ft longer! On 15th March, it was handed over to the engineers in charge of experimental vehicles and placed into service at Digbeth and then in June at Bearwood.

During the design stage, concern had been expressed regarding the ability of the 5-speed manual gearbox to cope with the increased torque output of the uprated 10.5 litre engine. An approach had been made to Self Chang-

ing Gears Ltd (SCG) as to whether they had a suitable 5-speed overdrive, semi-automatic gearbox. At that time, in late 1961, they did not have a suitable unit. In April 1963, a prototype unit became available. As a result, the prototype CM6T was withdrawn from service and the SCG gearbox installed. Initial development testing showed that, as supplied, the gear change quality was not acceptable and a number of modifications were carried out in conjunction with SCG.

By the end of August 1963, the prototype CM6T had completed 22,000 miles in service with no major problems. The following month the coach was withdrawn from service for various body alterations and some mechanical updates. The coach returned to motorway service at the end of April 1964 and continued to be monitored by the Development Department. It was subsequently allocated to Rugby garage in February 1965, where it would go on to spend most of its working life. In the aforementioned refurbishment, the lantern windscreen gave way to a slightly inclined screen consisting of four sections, the corner pieces being curved. The door was only partly glazed and made to open inwards, necessitating the removal of the wrap-around bumper moulding, which had previously spanned the bottom of the door. Ventilation on the CM6T did not include the C5's window hoppers and was therefore reliant on forced airflow, using a system developed with Smiths Industries. To aid the efficiency of this system, scoops were now fitted on the roof above the first window bay. Internally the seating was reduced to 44, with a luggage rack placed across the back alongside the toilet. The tin toilet with hand pump (of the Elsan variety), which had been used on the CM5T, was replaced by an electrically flushed toilet.

In 1964, a start was made on the production batch of 29 vehicles. Mechanically they were to be like the final version of the prototype, but the appearance was remodelled again and the resemblance to the C5 was definitely severed.

The body was built with six bays, having wider pillar spacing between the windows (the prototype had seven bays). The front and rear were restyled and the roof was made to dip at each end finishing in 'peaks' fore and aft. These peaks were not just for style but had streamlining characteristics. Two of the three roof lights opened, activated electronically, although later, through lack of maintenance, these became problematical. The route boards above the side windows, which had been carried over from the CM5 to the prototype, were now replaced by four yellow perspex destination displays which could be illuminated from behind. The waistline, which had hitherto sloped down ahead of the forward side win-

dow, was replaced by a step. Once more, the saloon ventilation system was modified with the air scoops being moved back along the roof to above the sixth main bay. These were flat box-like affairs, which were altered yet again

BMMO CM6T PROTOTYPE SPECIFICATION (as at August 1963)

ENGINE
BMMO Horizontal 10.5 litre, naturally aspirated.
Bore   4.880 in.
Stroke 5.709 in.
Compression ratio 16:1.
142 bhp at 1950 rpm.

CLUTCH
Single dry-plate, 15⅞ in. diameter.

GEARBOX
Self Changing Gears RV61 semi-automatic epicyclic.
Gear ratios:

First	4.28:1
Second	2.43:1
Third	1.64:1
Fourth	1:1 (direct)
Fifth	0.74:1 (overdrive)
Reverse	5.97:1

REAR AXLE
Fully floating unit with Kirkstall hypoid-bevel drive.
Ratio 4.44:1.

BRAKES
BMMO-Girling disc brakes with Lockheed continuous-flow-powered hydraulic system, in conjunction with Lockheed tandem accumulator system, giving 4:1 servo effect, operating on front and rear wheels. Mechanically operated transmission handbrake, 16 in. diameter disc type, with cable-operated bi-sector unit.

SUSPENSION
Metalastik variable-rate rubber suspension front and rear. Inclined bonded sandwich units at front, and double torsional toggle links at rear. Independent front suspension, trailing arm and upper wishbone system. Rear suspension adjustable for height. Armstrong telescopic dampers at all wheels.

STEERING
Marles double-cam steering box. Ratio 28.5:1.

TYRES
Front 10.00x20 in. 14 ply; rear 9.00x20 in. 10 ply.

ELECTRICAL
24-volt starting and lighting equipment, four 6-volt 135-amp-hr batteries.

FRAME
All steel welded construction integral with body.

BODY ITEMS

Dimensions	Overall length	36ft 0 in.
	Overall width	8ft 2½ in.
	Front overhang	7ft 0 in.
	Wheel base	18ft 7 in.
	Rear overhang	10ft 5 in.
Windows	14 side windows.	
	Lantern type windscreen.	
Heating	3 heaters Smiths recirculatory unit type R551	
Ventilation	Smiths-BMMO forced air system to individual jet vents.	
Seats	46 coachbuilt seats.	
Toilet	Compartment at rear nearside. Chemical type.	
Unladen Weight	8 tons 0 cwt 0 qr. Distribution 3 tons 10 cwt 2 qr on front wheels, 4 tons 9 cwt 2 qr on rear wheels.	

Opposite page:

Top: **The BMMO CM6T Motorway Coach.**

Bottom left and right: **With the exception of the one-off S19 bus, all BMMO-built single-deckers from the S14 onwards, used the same Metalastik rubber suspension system.**

A.J. Hurst designed the system for Coventry-based Metalastik. The use of rubber suspension on buses was considered quite revolutionary when it appeared on the first S14 in 1953.

The front suspension unit, which consisted of three layers of rubber bonded to metal plates, acted as a spring in place of the more conventional leaf spring. The path of the wheel movement was controlled by the geometry of the linkage. The bottom transverse link is longer than the one situated at the top. This was done to prevent any transverse wheel movement of the road wheel during deflection.

On the rear suspension, each suspension unit consisted of two metal and rubber bonded bushes with the outer sleeve of each connected together by four toggle-links. These toggle-link units located the axle, the height of the vehicle body being adjusted by the diagonal turnbuckle.

The rubber used on this system was available in varying degrees of stiffness. These different types were colour coded. Blue rubber was used on buses and standard coaches, but the motorway coaches, which required a firmer ride, had red rubber.

at a later production stage, becoming larger and, as they followed the roof curve, more stylish. Practically, this rear position afforded more space for the ventilation fans and filters. The original forward location for these was inhibited by the destination box, first aid box and the passenger door. It had also been found that the original position of the scoops spoiled the body streamlining. Once again, the passenger door was glazed in two sections. It opened inwards in such a way that the exterior side was away from the alighting/embarking passenger, muddy or wet contact being avoided! A retractable step was provided beneath the emergency door.

John Morris was a Management Trainee with Midland Red during 1964-1966. He recalls the road-testing of the new CM6Ts then being built at Central Works.

'I was a passive 17-year-old observer witnessing some of this testing. On several occasions two young engineers in white dustcoats, accompanied by myself, would board a body-finished vehicle painted in green primer and without interior fittings. It ran on trade plates. It was loaded with a number of 56lb weights to form a second floor covering. There was a large sofa placed behind the cab area, which provided 'luxurious' comfort for the observers. Off we would go on a 1,000 miles road test.

'This would involve driving from Birmingham to the start of the M6 Motorway near Junction 13 at Dunston, near Stafford, and then going full pelt up the motorway at speeds of up to 100 mph all the way to Charnock Richard services in Lancashire.[45] I kid you not regarding the speed! Don't forget this was in the 1960s and traffic on the M6 was very light; we simply stayed in the empty right hand lane all the way! I vividly remember drivers of sports cars, probably doing 80 mph, looking at us open-mouthed as this large green machine drifted past them.'

When it was pointed out to John that these coaches had a speedo which only went up to 80 mph, he replied: 'I don't know about

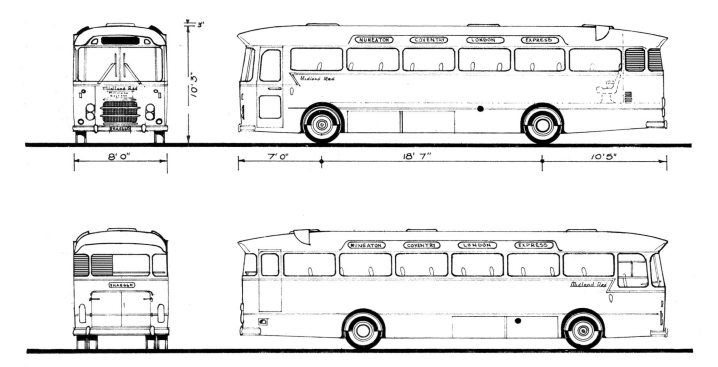

Notes

45 Jim Pearson has something to say about this! 'If I had still been Development Engineer at that time, these engineers would have got the rough edge of my tongue concerning their 1,000 mile bedding-in and test procedure. The purpose of the 1,000 mile test was to gently bed in the engine and transmission units by gradually increasing the vehicle speed over a period of many miles. To go full pelt as soon as they got on to the motorway was definitely not part of the agenda. Any traffic driver could have filled that role.'

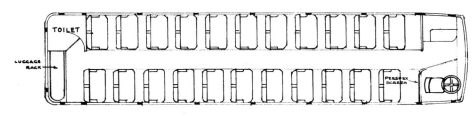

Front Suspension

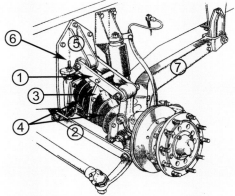

① UPPER WISHBONES
② LOWER WISHBONES
③ INTERMEDIATE STEADY PLATE
④ METALASTIK RUBBER SUSPENSION UNITS
⑤ FRAME MOUNTING BRACKET
⑥ SUSPENSION HEIGHT ADJUSTER SCREWS
⑦ LONGITUDINAL LOCATION RADIUS ROD

Rear Suspension

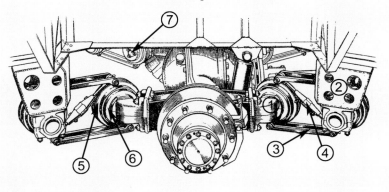

① AXLE MOUNTING BRACKET
② FRAME MOUNTING BRACKET
③ LINKS
④ TOGGLE ADJUSTER (TURNBUCKLE)
⑤ OUTER SLEEVE
⑥ RUBBER BUSH
⑦ INNER SLEEVE (HIDDEN BEHIND END PLATE)

Another shot of 5295, following some restyling. Note the flat windscreen and partly glazed passenger door. It was photographed on its way to Victoria with CM5T 4809 behind. BaMMOT

the speedo used on the service-ready CM6s. I clearly remember one day, when the engineer driver whooped as he told us that we were doing 100 mph. The other engineer and I joined in the cheering! Perhaps the vehicles had a test speedo fitted. They certainly had a number of other engineering test items on board, which they loaded on for each trip. I cannot remember for sure, but these items would almost certainly include the engineer's oil pressure and temperature gauges and as mentioned previously, the vehicles were not fully fitted out, so the speedo could well have been a test engineer's fitment. I further recall that we occasionally stopped by the roadside

as some item or other needed adjustment. Don't forget that these vehicles were still in mid-development in early 1965 and these guys would try anything to improve the vehicles!

'At Charnock Richard, we would have a pleasant lunch and then back to Birmingham. After minor adjustments, this trip would be repeated the next day, until 1,000 miles had been covered. Once the testing was completed, the CM6T would be passed fit for service and handed over to the final assembly people for fitment of interior and painting. I don't know if all the CM6Ts went through this process but my understanding was that it was a 'running in' routine of 1,000 miles.'

5646 was the first production CM6T and had an altogether new body. It was photographed at Central Works prior to delivery. BMMO

INTO SERVICE

In February 1965, a milestone for the Birmingham-London motorway service was reached. On the 19th of that month, a school teacher, Miss Marilyn Harrison, boarded the 2 o'clock departure from Digbeth. She was surprised to be greeted by a party of Midland Red officials. They informed her that she was the one mil-lionth passenger for that particular service. She was duly presented with a leather suitcase.

The same month saw the first production CM6T delivered to Bearwood garage, followed by another nine before the year was out and Digbeth also had three. All of these were for the Birmingham-London service.

Nuneaton garage had eight[46] delivered for their London service, these arriving between

Notes

46 5658 and 5660-66.

Seen when only a month old, CM6T 5653 getting up to speed on the M45 heading south. T W Moore

CM6T 5651 Birmingham-bound on the A45 Coventry by-pass in June 1966. It is being overtaken by a Ford Cortina and followed by a Bedford coach belonging to Cave's of Shirley, Solihull. Coaches were restricted to 50 mph on roads of this type. T W Moore

Top left: **CM6T 5657 London-bound on the A45 Coventry by-pass in June 1966.** T W Moore

Top right: **CM6T 5653 returning to Birmingham, photographed on the A45 Coventry by-pass in June 1966.** T W Moore

Above: **The second production CM6T was delivered to Bearwood in April 1965, and is seen leaving there the following month to take up service from Digbeth Coach Station.** Ken Jubb

Right: **A fresh load of passengers arrive in London aboard CM6T 5655.** R H G Simpson

CM6T 5673 engaged on a non-motorway duty, travels along High Street, Digbeth. A J Willis

From 1967, coaches started to appear with maroon roofs in place of the long-established black, as seen here on CM6T 5672. Ken Jubb

Part of Midland Red's anti-nationalisation campaign is seen on the rather nicely produced roof board carried by CM6T 5669. Nevertheless, Midland Red passed into government ownership in 1968. BMMO

October 1965 and February 1966. It is worth noting that, unlike the earlier motorway coaches used on the Nuneaton-Coventry-London service, a toilet was now provided.

A toilet-less variant (CM6), configured as a 46 seater, was built but this was for the Birmingham-Worcester service. Four of these went to Worcester garage and one to Digbeth.[47] These were delivered between March and May 1966. The final three CM6Ts built went to Digbeth in May 1966.

Following delivery the new coaches were soon hard at work. Drivers were more than happy with them and though in appearance they were perhaps more workmanlike than some other body designs currently entering the arena, they were still out in front performance-wise and doing the business.

Ex-Midland Red driver Mike Holloway recalls how colleagues claimed 100 mph speeds on occasion with the CM5. 'Certainly we got near that on the CM6Ts; especially on the downhill stretch at Luton bank, we were off the clock. There, it was only the engine holding us back. Some drivers put the coach into neutral to get even more speed, but I never tried that!' Indeed, such bad driving practice would have been frowned upon by the Engineering Department, because putting the SCG box into neutral in this manner would have interfered with the internal lubrication system of the gearbox.

Drivers on motorway work had a privileged job and the pay was good. Prospective drivers were given a company medical, a theory test on the motorway section of the Highway Code and a practical test on motorway coach work. Mike Holloway again, 'All the training was based on the Bearwood garage. When I was tested, we had to take a coach from Digbeth up the M6 to Stoke and back. After that, if successful and passed as "Motorway Safe", we were given coach work and some duplicated motorway service work. Later, we would do regular motorway work, but the amount varied with the season.'

Mike frequently did the evening service to London which positioned him for the first one out of London the following day. He continues, 'Contract lodgings were provided by the company plus a subsistence allowance. When a duplicate coach was needed, then it fell to the driver to find accommodation. If inexpensive lodgings were all fully booked, drivers would sleep in the coach and then avail themselves of the wash and brush-up facilities at Victoria Coach Station, where breakfast would be taken. We used overnight coach parking near Westminster Abbey. It was on a one-time bombsite, I think. It had been levelled out at cellar depth and made into an overspill coach park. You accessed it by going down a ramp. There was a similar arrangement at Battersea.'

When the West Midlands Passenger Transport Executive (WMPTE) took over many of the Midland Red garages, buses and staff located within the West Midlands conurbation, Digbeth, which remained 'Red', became the company's 'Coach Unit' and all drivers were needed to man the influx of coaches transferred there.

In 1974, Lloyd Penfold was an experienced bus and coach driver. He had only worked for Midland Red at Digbeth, on a full-time basis, for a matter of weeks when he was told he would be on coach work, which would include motorway services. This was a sign of the times, for as has been related already, the position of coach driver, let alone a motorway coach driver, was only bestowed after some years of unblemished service. Lloyd was hardly able to believe his good fortune.

'I was told to learn the Motorway Express route. The man who was showing me, Bernard Morris, a former Sutton driver and inspector, believed the best way to learn a route was to drive it.

'Now, there had been a tradition of seniority in the Midland Red, dating back to its earliest days, where decades could be taken progressing from bus to coach driving, and even longer waiting for the promotion to motorway driver. However, this was all swept away when I, who had only been full-time for about ten days, sat at the wheel of a CM6T motorway express coach and pulled out of Digbeth bound for London.

'To be at the helm of a CM6 in full flight is a wondrous thing. Remember, these were the days before restrictions on speed and usage of outside lanes on motorways were more rigid, and the traffic was much lighter than it is now.

'Down the Aston Expressway and onto the M6 I went, building up to a respectable 70 mph by Fort Dunlop, when Bernard said, "It's warmed up now; lift your foot about a quarter of an inch on the throttle." I did, and gradually the speed built up and I was passing everything, the speedo needle way past its maximum display of 80. I was hooked - King of the road!'

ROUTES

Midland Red attempted to operate a fourth motorway service when, in November 1965, the M1 was extended northwards into Leicestershire. Doubtless, this would have been operated by the CM5 or new CM6Ts. The proposed route was Burton-upon-Trent via Swadlincote, Woodville, Ashby, Coalville and Markfield, joining the M1 near Markfield and on to Victoria Coach Station, London. Journey time was to be 3 hours 20 minutes. Weekday services were just one journey each way, with additional journeys offered over the weekend period (Friday pm - Monday am). A detailed timetable and fares listing was published and circulated in the catchment area. On the flip side of this leaflet was a letter from General Manager, Donald Sinclair, encouraging would-be passengers to write to Midland Red (using the Business Reply Card provided), stating why the service would be of benefit to them. Viking Motors Burton Ltd was also seeking the same licence. In the event, both were refused. Later, a summer Saturday service ran as route ME8 and then, later still, a joint service with Viking Coaches.

Routes were modified as motorways were extended or access to them improved, but time saved here was often counterbalanced by lost time through road works. The Birmingham-Selly Oak-Worcester service was assigned the route number X44 and used the Bristol Road out of Birmingham to the motorway. When the M5 was extended another six miles northwards and the junction at Quinton opened on 19th November 1965, alternate services joined the M5 via the Hagley Road, routing Birmingham-Bearwood-Worcester and this service

was given the route number X43. The X44 now stopped at Northfield as well as Selly Oak.

Meanwhile, the Birmingham-London service had become route ME1. The Coventry service which, as already mentioned, had been quickly extended to include Nuneaton, was identified as route ME2.

In November 1971, the section of the M6 Motorway linking Gravelly Hill, Birmingham, with the M1 Motorway at Junction 19 (Catthorpe), was completed. This was followed by the opening of the Aston Expressway (A38M) in May 1972. Coaches on the ME1 could now take this route instead of the A45/M45. It was longer by five miles but found to be quicker, as the amount of non-motorway travel was reduced by 25 miles.

Also, with the expanding motorway network, other Midland Red services were highlighting their use of the motorways. These were hardly express services and had numerous intermediate pick-up points, but the following featured in a 1969 timetable:

ME3	Coventry-Birmingham-Glasgow (Daily in Summer, weekends in Winter. Joint with other operators).
ME4	Birmingham-Coventry-East Kent resorts (Summer Saturdays only. Joint with East Kent).
ME5	Birmingham-Coventry-London-Brighton-Worthing (Summer Saturdays only. Joint with Southdown).
ME6	Birmingham-Coventry-London-Eastbourne (Summer Saturdays only. Joint with Southdown).
ME7	Shrewsbury-Wolverhampton-Sutton Coldfield-Yardley-London (Weekends only).
ME8	Burton-Swadlincote-Woodville-Ashby-Coalville-Markfield-London (Summer Saturdays only).

One of the last CM6Ts to be delivered was 5674. It was subsequently restyled in 1972, as seen in this photograph taken at Digbeth. The route number M6 is presumably an alternative way of presenting the Coventry-Glasgow route ME3.
Ken Jubb

Displaying route ME3 is
CM6T 5652, caught here
at Hamilton Bus Station in
June 1973. A J Douglas

In addition, a timetable from 1971 also showed the following service as being via the motorway: Redditch-Stratford upon Avon-Banbury-Milton Keynes-London (Weekends only).

It is possible that CM6Ts may have found their way on to such services, but if they did, it would most likely have been late in their careers.

Lloyd Penfold, recalling his early motorway driving at the start of 1974, says, 'CM6Ts were used on the Coventry-Birmingham-Wolverhampton-Glasgow run but only if Midland Red drivers were used throughout. There was a meal break taken at Forton services, Lancaster. Some duties not involving the CM6Ts were operated on a "kiss and turn" basis, where a Western Scottish driver would bring his coach southbound to Forton and return north with the Midland Red one, the "Red" driver bringing the WSMT coach south. Personally I hated those because WSMT used Leyland Leopards or Seddon Pennines, limited to 55 mph, the Seddons more so, as with Gardner engines, they had a very heavy right pedal.'

In the latter months of the CM6Ts, even before National Express introduced its 500 series of route numbers,[48] coaches could be seen simply displaying the road to be used (e.g. ME1 displayed M1 and ME3 displayed M6). Mike Holloway explains, 'When we had the big destination boxes on the restyled vehicles, it was left to the driver as to what he showed in the number tracks. He was only required to show the place of destination. So some drivers might show the actual route number, say ME2, others might put up M1, as that would be just as informative, if not more so!'

A Piece Of Cake!

To continue the ME3 Glasgow theme, John Seale relates an anecdote passed onto him by the late George Foster, an ex-Midland Red driver. George relayed the story when presenting his own driver's white smock, as a momento, to John. George hated wearing this smock and draped it over his seat, once out of sight of those who might take him to task.

George was a Digbeth-based CM6 driver. On one occasion, he was driving his coach on the M6 heading for Glasgow, when an army lorry driven by a learner appeared in front of him. The learner driver should not have been on the motorway. He must have realised his predicament and panicked. Signalling left but actually veering right toward the fast lane, he was moving into the path of George's oncoming CM6T.

In a split second, George knew he could not avoid the slow-moving lorry and knowing that his passengers must be his first concern, he

Notes

48 For example ME1 became 501 and ME2 became 502.

looked at the central reservation crash barrier and elected to use it to bring the coach to a rapid stop. He went through it and then over it. The vertical barrier posts, engaging with the underside of the CM6T, stopped it more quickly than a brake application, which would have been harder to control.

Amidst the tearing of metal, the windscreen disappeared and in the silence that followed, George, somewhat shaken, got out of his seat to attend to his passengers. An irate Scots woman berated him for losing the Dundee cake that she had baked for her sister. The tin and its contents had streaked up the motorway. It transpired that the cake had been on a parcel rack and, upon impact, it had continued travelling. It was this that had taken out the windscreen. George said it was all the fuss about the cake that relieved the tension, as his passengers thanked him for a lucky escape!

FINAL PHASE

CM6T 5654 entered the company's Central Works in early 1971 for modification and in May emerged as the sole example of the CM6A. It had been fitted with a large bus-style destination box, a power-operated door and one-man-operation equipment, and had lost much of its exterior trim. It was finished in overall red and generally thought to be a blot on the marque. It spent a few months in service at Worcester. It was returned to CM6 standard, losing the one-man-operation equipment, and was given a fresh facelift, before re-entering service from Bearwood in May 1972.

A project commencing in January 1972 and finishing in May 1973, saw 18 CM6Ts enter Central Works for overhaul and restyling. This time the result was far better than the CM6A effort. As with the CM6A, a large destina-

tion box was fitted to the front dome. Deep polished waist mouldings were fitted and looked particularly striking at the front end, whilst the floor level moulding was extended around the front across the radiator grille and the lights/indicators moved accordingly. Roof lights were reduced to two (manually opened) fore and aft.

Mike Holloway comments, 'We reckoned that the big destination box cost us about 10 mph, but we quite liked the polished mouldings. I was also pleased that the maroon roof was gone.[49] These modified coaches came back to us in all-over red. Prior to the refurbishment, the coaches had got pretty smelly. The carpet had been difficult to keep clean and that was now replaced by a sort of lino. To our embarrassment, leaks from the toilet system had rotted the floor and waste would run into the boot and on to the luggage. The boot apron would get detached, then lost, and the seals let in rain and dirt on to the unprotected luggage. So we were glad to get these re-born vehicles!'

Despite this work the coaches were not to last much longer. They had all done very high mileages and it has been said that some spares had become impossible to procure. As early as February 1972 suitably modified Leyland Leopards, classed as CM7As, had taken over the M5 Birmingham-Worcester services.[50]

In 1972, some of the CM6 class were being demoted to less demanding work. This included limited-stop services and long-distance routes, which were operated in conjunction with other bus companies. Still others were being withdrawn, the first four going in July 1972. Upon withdrawal, a number were stored at Worcester and Cradley Heath garages.

Notes

49 See Appendix A.

50 Just why the CM6s came off this service is far from clear. The vehicles went to Digbeth and Nuneaton; two even being restyled. The CM7As were very unpopular with staff and had to be supplemented with S24 Leopards to maintain the X43/44 service. The situation was eased the following year with the arrival of the dual-purpose S27 Leopards.

Making for a good comparison, CM6T 5664 alongside restyled CM6T 5674.
Travel Lens Photographic

A shortage of spares and poor maintenance dogged many of the CM6 class at the end of their lives. However, CM6T 5657 was in trouble in the late 1960s. It is being towed by S9 (tree cutter) 3374, which also appears to have its problems. Andrew Hawthorn collection

Top: **When the CM6s were taken off the Birmingham-Worcester service, 5667 moved to Digbeth. Here, it is on a trip to Bristol via Cheltenham.** Transport Museum, Wythall collection

Centre: **On Friday 31st August 1973, there must have been a shortage of buses at Digbeth garage because CM6T 5665 found itself on the 159 Coventry-Birmingham route, much to the delight of Mike Greenwood, who travelled on it and took this photograph.**

Bottom left: **CM6 5668 left Worcester and, after a spell at Digbeth, it was restyled and repainted, arriving at Nuneaton in May 1973. It is seen here at Coventry.** Transport Museum, Wythall collection

Bottom right: **The white livery did not lend itself well to motorway work, as exemplified by CM6T 5656.** Omnicolour

Restyled vehicles continued to grace the M1 Motorway until the final withdrawals, indeed a mass exodus, occurred in April 1974. A batch of 20 Leyland PSU3B/4RT Leopards, with 44-seat Plaxton bodies (complete with toilet), arrived to continue the work. These new coaches were in National Bus Company white livery, which had also been applied to some of the CM6 class, the first of which was 5652 in June 1972.

An observation from Mike Holloway, 'Midland Red had enjoyed a "presence" on the motorway from the beginning. Headlight-flashing and intimidation were hardly needed; cars and lorries saw the red coach in their mirror and moved over. When we had the NBC livery, we seemed to lose that edge. We were just another white coach.'

Midland Red was no longer the bus company/builder at the leading edge, but just one of the segments which made up NBC. However, Midland Red had accrued a marvellous record of achievements. It had pioneered and then, for almost 15 years, run motorway express services in vehicles it had designed and built at its own works facility. Now, sadly the era was over.

Only three of the CM6Ts saw further use after Midland Red, 5656, 5662 and 5663. The first of these was acquired for preservation in 1975 by a group of Midland Red enthusiasts, based at Leamington Spa. Three years later, it was in the care of BaMMOT, now referred to as the Transport Museum, Wythall. It took to the road again in October 2009, the first time in 15 years. The other two coaches did not have more than the odd few months with various operators. These included Thos. Morris and Son of Pencoed, and Everton of Droitwich. BaMMOT obtained 5662 for spares in 1984. In 2000, a group of enthusiasts acquired this vehicle and have kept it undercover in Staffordshire, but a good deal of effort and money will be needed to make it presentable.

NBC introduced new route numbers for the motorway services in 1973. CM6T 5674 is displaying route 501, as it leaves Victoria for Digbeth, in October 1973. A J Douglas

Towards the end of their working lives, less pride was taken in the appearance of the vehicles. CM6T 5653 has a white painted wheel, obviously taken off another vehicle with NBC livery. Photobus

Above: **This picture shows five CM6Ts at Digbeth in May 1974, a month after their withdrawal from service. Someone seems to have been having a little fun, with the number blinds displaying local works service numbers.** Mike Greenwood

Right: **The replacement for the CM6Ts was the formidable Leyland Leopard with its Plaxton Elite III body. It was designated type C14 by Midland Red, who took delivery of 20 examples, this one being fleet number 310 (PHA 310M).** A Homer

Below: **Only two CM6Ts saw further commercial use, 5662 and 5663. Both vehicles spent a few months working with Thos. Morris of Pencoed. Pictured here is former 5662.** Ken Jubb

Below right: **When Thos. Morris sold the two CM6Ts, they went to Everton of Droitwich. 5663 is seen here when with the latter company.** Ken Jubb

LIVERY

As there were always exceptions to the rule, documenting liveries carried by vehicles covered in this book is potentially problematical. These tended to occur when vehicles changed role, or when a new scheme was introduced and some vehicles, near the end of their service lives, may not have been given the full make over.

When delivered, all C5, CM5T, CM5, CM6T and CM6 coaches wore the standard Midland Red coach livery of bright red with black roof. As mentioned in the main text, from 1963 a large white panel was painted on the roof to reflect heat. This was not visible at ground level.

The C5 variants had a polished aluminium-scripted *Midland Red* badge above the radiator grille. There was also a gold logo; this consisted of the 'Midland Red' title within an oval, flanked by 'wings'. This logo had been used on the S15 dual-purpose buses and looked stylish. Initially, it appeared on both sides of the body and boot. Early on, the boot presentation was simplified to show just the fleet name. Presumably, the winged oval was deemed inappropriate, giving as it did the impression of sideways travel! Above the boot handle was the fleet number and above the rear bumper the mandatory seating capacity information, both in gold.

A staged publicity photo shows the standard livery for the CM5T coaches. BMMO

The first few C5s had the full logo on the boot. This was soon modified so that only the fleet name appeared. BMMO

Right: **From 1967, the black roof gave way to maroon. 4791 is seen here at Llandudno.**
Andrew Hawthorn collection

Below left: **A number of C5As found their way into service still wearing their coach livery. 4831 is seen here at Coventry on a football excursion in April 1968.**
Patrick Kingston

Below right: **Official livery for the C5A buses was overall red with fleet name presentation appropriate for the period. 4826 is seen here at Leamington Spa in the winter of 1970-1971.**
Ken Jubb

Bottom: **CM6Ts were delivered in the standard red with black roof livery. Here, 5651 is seen at Worcester alongside S16, 5111, in May 1967.** Christopher Davis

Other legal lettering was 'Emergency Door' in gold; unladen weight in white, displayed low down ahead of the nearside rear wheel (typically UW 6 18 1 for a CM5T), and company-contact details in black, low down behind the nearside front wheel *viz*

THE BIRMINGHAM & MIDLAND MOTOR OMNIBUS Co. Ltd.
MIDLAND HOUSE, VERNON ROAD, BIRMINGHAM.
D.M. SINCLAIR M.I. Mech.E. M.Inst. T.
GENERAL MANAGER

In 1967, there was a new General Manager, J.W. WOMAR. In the same year, but not necessarily connected, the long-established red and black coach livery was changed to red with maroon roof, the white panel being retained.

The CM5(T)s had wooden route boards above the saloon windows. On the first motorway coaches these boards, which were red with gold lettering, read: BIRMINGHAM-LONDON MOTORWAY EXPRESS

On the flip side and one assumes to offer flexibility was: MIDLAND "RED" MOTOR SERVICES

The boards on the CM5s for the Coventry service read: COVENTRY-LONDON MOTORWAY EXPRESS

Later, when the service was extended the boards were lengthened to read: NUNEATON-COVENTRY-LONDON MOTORWAY EXPRESS

Boards for CM5s on the Worcester service read: BIRMINGHAM-SELLY OAK-WORCESTER EXPRESS

The less specific Midland "Red" Motor Services boards appeared also on non-motorway coaches i.e. on some C5s and CS5s.

The 45 C5A buses were, in the main (*see photo of 4831 opposite as an exception*), painted red all over, with the gold fleet name MIDLAND in quite small upper case letters, appearing on the body sides. Some seem to have run with no fleet name. Other C5As were around long enough to receive the yellow with black outline (1971) style **Midland Red**.

The CM6(T)s mirrored the same colours as their older brothers but did not have the gold fleet name logo on the side or rear. Instead, the fleet name was in polished aluminium across the radiator grille. Alternatively, the fleet name was beneath the windscreen, together with the similarly scripted words *Motorway Express*, attached in the form of a polished aluminium badge. The scripted *Midland Red* wording was also carried on the sides under the forward passenger window and across the boot doors. The

This page:

When the restyled CM6Ts emerged from Central Works, they were painted overall red and, with their additional brightwork, looked most attractive. Omnicolour

The first of the CM6Ts to receive the NBC white livery was 5652, seen here at Digbeth in early summer 1972. It has the fleet name in silver and the NATIONAL name and logo was still to be applied. Ken Jubb

Three of the non-restyled CM6Ts, along with this CM6, 5667, appeared in the NBC white livery. This Digbeth-based coach is bound for Bristol. Ken Jubb

Opposite page:

CM6T 5666 in full NBC livery. Note the side perspex panels which read 'Midland-Red-London-Express'. Ken Jubb

Two restyled CM6Ts make for a good comparison of liveries. 5665 is in red and 5666 in white. Omnicolour

fleet number appeared on the boot also, straddling the centre line of the doors.

Route boards were not fitted. In place of these were four backlit yellow perspex panels, each displaying a single word in black. On the first CM6Ts these read:

BIRMINGHAM LONDON MOTORWAY EXPRESS
or
NUNEATON COVENTRY LONDON EXPRESS
or on the CM6s
BIRMINGHAM WORCESTER MOTORWAY EXPRESS

Later, there was a number of other four word combinations.

When the restyled CM6Ts emerged from Central Works, they were in overall red, and with their additional polished trim looked very attractive. Fleet name **Midland Red,** in the form of a transfer, was in silver coloured letters above the radiator grille and the same, although underlined, on either side, below the forward passenger window and repeated on the boot. The fleet number, also in silver, was now displayed below the centre of the windscreen as well as on the boot.

From June 1972, the NBC white livery started to appear on the CM6(T)s and did not suit them, especially the ones which had not been restyled. The fleet name was in red and carried beneath the forward passenger side windows. On the sides towards the back was the word **NATIONAL** in large capital letters, together with the NBC logo in red and blue. The fleet number was still carried on the front

and rear in silver. Some had a metal badge fixed to the radiator grille, displaying the NBC logo.

At this stage, 1972-1974, a number of variations in detail occurred. These were especially evident as vehicles (some restyled, others not) were repainted white.

Other small variations might occur when these coaches came off motorway work and did less demanding duties, these included longer-distance bus routes.

In conclusion, few will argue that the first livery of red and black was best and especially suited the C5 class. The NBC policy of painting all coaches white, irrespective of whatever fleet they belonged to, and then displaying the fleet name e.g. Midland Red, or Royal Blue, or Red and White, was not inspiring.

COMMEMORATIVE RUNS

The significance of the opening of Britain's first major motorway and Midland Red's Birmingham-London motorway service has been marked by a series of commemorative re-runs.

The first of these was Friday 2nd November 1979, celebrating the 20th anniversary. By that time BMMO had become the Midland Red Omnibus Company (MROC) and it was this company which organised the event. The coach used was CM6T, fleet number 5656, which was in preservation in the care of the Birmingham and Midland Motor Omnibus Trust (BaMMOT). A contemporary Leyland Leopard with Plaxton Supreme IV body accompanied it. The Leyland had only been registered the previous day. The driver for the CM6T was Lloyd Penfold, who was still employed by Midland Red at that time and has already shared some of his experiences in this book. The Leyland was driven by Ernie Hawkins, who was intimately acquainted with CM6T 5656, claiming to have driven it in service at 92 mph.

The pair of coaches left Digbeth Coach Station at 10:00 hours and, because of time restrictions, did not use the original A45/M45 route to reach the M1, but the later one, which used the A38M/M6. An ATV camera crew was on the older coach. A 15-minute stop was made at Corley services so that photographs could be taken and the camera crew transferred to the Leyland. Arrival at Victoria Coach Station was still only three hours after departing from Digbeth, even though the CM6T never exceeded 67 mph. The return trip was blighted by heavy traffic and the engine was showing signs of what turned out to be fuel starvation.

Two days later on Sunday 4th November, the trip was repeated with 5656, this being specifically for BaMMOT members. This time the engine did suffer fuel supply problems on the outward leg, necessitating roadside repairs in a lay-by on the A45.

The 30th anniversary was celebrated on Thursday 2nd November 1989, and by now it was National Express who hosted the event. The historic coach this time was C5 4819, which was owned by Dave Whitelaw of Sutton Coldfield. The vehicle had only just been made roadworthy. Along with other things it had been necessary to repair a cracked block. Dave Whitelaw drove the coach out of Digbeth at 09:20 hours and headed off towards the M1 via the A45/M45. On a very wet M1, cruising was at a relatively sedate 55 mph and a number of stops were made to top up the radiator. The journey to Victoria took four hours. National Express provided an escort in the shape of a Volvo B10M Expressliner with a Plaxton Paramount III body, making the C5 look quite small.

The third run occurred on a beautifully sunny Tuesday 2nd November 1999. Once again C5 4819 was the coach to carry on the tradition. By now it was in the hands of the South Staffordshire Heritage Bus Co. and was leased by National Express for the occasion. National Express was also able to provide a driver, one Mike Holloway, who, it will be recalled, had worked for Midland Red driving CM6Ts - Mike wore his original coach driver's white hat and coat. Passengers for the run included members of the press, invited guests from the days of Midland Red (including Bob Richards who is also mentioned earlier in this book) and some passengers who had been on the inaugural service in 1959.

Once again, the route taken was as close as possible to that used originally. At the time Mike Holloway reported, 'Using the relative quiet of the M45 near Coventry, we were able to take the old lady up to 70 mph, but on the M1, because we are no longer permitted in the outside lane, we were hindered by lorries. Nonetheless, we moved comfortably at 60-65 mph. We had the usual traffic in London, but the journey time was a creditable three hours.'

On arrival at Victoria, the engineer's eye of Bob Richards spotted an oil leak. Upon inspection over the pits at nearby Samuelsons, this turned out to be a pin hole in the sump. This was fixed by screwing in a self-tapper covered with sealant. The coach and passengers were then taken to the London Transport Museum at Covent Garden for a specially laid-on

The first commemorative run took place on 2nd November 1979, using CM6T 5656 which was, by that stage, in the care of the Birmingham and Midland Motor Omnibus Trust. It was joined by a Leyland Leopard with Plaxton Supreme body of National Express.
Alan Watkins

luncheon and a look around the display halls.

The return journey was made in the dark. 'It was a great atmosphere to be driving in the dark and with the original interior lights on. The headlamps were fine, as was everything about the vehicle. Prior to the trip, the owners had changed the tyres and got the brakes well adjusted. Everything was as it should be,' said Mike.

The most recent celebration was on Saturday 31st October 2009 and fittingly, for the 50th year, both a C5 and CM6T made the trip. Roger Burdett's long-anticipated restoration of C5 4780 was ready to go and was joined by BaMMOT's CM6T. Understandably, much interest was shown in 4780. However, the CM6T deserved its share of the limelight. The latter had not been on the road since 1994 and there was much work done during 2009 by the volunteers at the Transport Museum, Wythall (BaMMOT), before it was presented for its Class 5 certification in October 2009.

National Express again was host but no longer at the traditional venue, as the old Digbeth Coach Station had closed in November 2008. The two coaches were joined at the temporary Birmingham Central Coach Station (sited opposite the old one) by National Express Scania K340 EB6/Caetano Levante.

The route was again via the A45/M45 and, as in 1979, Lloyd Penfold was at the wheel of CM6T 5656 and Roger Burdett drove his C5 4780. Departure was at 09:00 hours and, with a stop en-route, the journey was three and a half hours. In London, the convoy travelled down Oxford Street and around Hyde Park, before arriving on time at Victoria Coach Station. Leaving London at 14:30 hours, the coaches arrived back in Birmingham, without incident, around 18:00 hours. What a pity C5 4819 was not able to make the date.

C5 4819 made both the 1989 and 1999 commemorative runs. It was photographed here leaving Digbeth Coach Station on the second of these dates. Author

Mike Holloway, dressed for the occasion, with 4819 on 2nd November 1999. Author

Fittingly for the 50th anniversary run, two historic vehicles were available. Photographed in Victoria Coach Station are C5 4780 and CM6T 5656. Dave Taylor

A superb photograph taken on the M45 Motorway, as a trio of coaches head back to Birmingham in the November twilight. 4780 leads with 5656 following and National Express Scania/Caetano bringing up the rear. David Hale

MINIATURES

An indication of just how Midland Red's motorway coach caught the public imagination is indicated by the attention given to the subject by toy manufacturers in the early 1960s. Two diecast and two plastic models were to be found on toy counters, whereas up until then the toy London bus had reigned supreme.

The best of these was the Corgi Toys example. Their CM5T was released in 1961 as part of the Major Toys range, with catalogue number 1120 and priced 8s 6d (43p). Its size was quite modest to be classed as a Major Toy; this category was usually for the likes of Bedford car transporters and petrol tankers, but it was a 'major' move forward in authenticity. It was modelled to 1/67th scale, and the accuracy for that period was very high; only the contemporary Corgi wheels letting it down. The model featured authentic transfers, independent suspension, plastic windows and interior (including the toilet compartment), whilst cast into the underside was a representation of the coach's mechanical attributes. Initially, it was packaged in a cardboard box with a pull-off lid; later the box was simplified to the end flap type.

Corgi's production ceased two years later and the only obvious variations on later models were the more accurate darker red and the use of chrome dish wheels to replace the dome wheels of the earlier ones.

Once Corgi had ceased production of the CM5T, Budgie Models Ltd produced their inferior diecast, catalogue number 296, between 1963 and 1966, which only had plastic windows and no other features of note save that it represented the twin headlights which were, by that stage, a feature of the real thing. It did have the advantage to railway modellers of being produced to OO scale and the box carried some comprehensive detail about Midland Red's motorway coach. A little-known fact is that there was an export version for the USA; this was painted with a light blue body and cream roof and carried the titles 'WASHINGTON D.C.' above the windows and below, 'BLUE LINE SIGHTSEEING CO.'

The plastic toys were made in Hong Kong and both had a friction motor. The smaller of the two was a scaled up (1/45th) clone of the Corgi Toy, using the same component mouldings. Whether this was done with Mettoy's consent (owners of Corgi) is not known. Aside from the 'Made in Hong Kong' legend, the only other identifier is the number '101'. This toy also appeared as a battery-powered remote-control version. This was done as a school bus

Corgi released their Midland Red motorway coach in 1961. Due to its authenticity, diecast toys began to cross over into the model collectors market, with many adults purchasing one at the cost of 8/6d.

Budgie's version of the CM5 coach was to 1/76th scale, but was not as popular as the Corgi Major Toy.

The Budgie version was also produced as a school bus for the American market.

An anonymous toy from Hong Kong, complete with friction motor, appeared in toy shops and is seen here alongside Corgi's version. Note that the former has been hand-painted by an enthusiast somewhere along the line.

The same anonymous plastic toy also came as an American school bus, this time with a battery-operated motor and hand-control.

An even larger plastic toy from Hong Kong was marketed by Guiterman. For size comparison it stands alongside Corgi's OOC model of the CM5T.

painted blue with a white roof, probably not for the UK market.

The other CM5T plastic toy, is to a very impressive 1/35th scale. As with the other plastic toy, the underside too has a representation of the mechanical units and also showed a reference number 'NF16'. Although made in Hong Kong, it was supplied by London-based Guiterman which, according to the box, was established in 1876. It is worth mentioning that Budgie was a part of the Guiterman group of companies.

Fast-forward nearly 40 years and allow the author to move into the first person. In 1998, I contacted Corgi Classics to point out that the following year would be the 40th anniversary of the opening of the M1 motorway and the introduction of the Midland Red CM5T. I suggested that they may wish to introduce a model to either the Classics 1/50th scale range or Original Omnibus Company (OOC) 1/76th series. I had had some contact with Corgi Collectors magazine for which I'd contributed a short article on the CM5T back in 1994. The suggestion fell on deaf ears. However, out of the blue in January 2000, I received a phone call from Corgi's Adrienne Fuller who wished to meet with me to discuss the variations and liveries which might be applied to an OOC model of the CM5! She had no knowledge of my suggestion which I had put forward two years earlier. It was apparent that she had seen my article on the subject which had appeared in *Classic Bus* magazine (No 43, October-November 1999) the previous autumn. The meeting took place and as a result I was given every encouragement to proceed with the gathering of the necessary reference material. This was with a view to releasing the first models in Spring of 2001. In addition, I also persuaded Adrienne of the virtues of modelling the BMMO D9 double-decker. The D9 project ran parallel to that of the C5 and for a similar release date.

Corgi draughtsman, Terry Fox, went to measure and photograph C5 4819, which at that time was in the hands of the South Staffordshire Heritage Bus Co, located at Cannock. The resulting model was not a disappointment.

Strangely, in my opinion, three models were released simultaneously in April 2001. These were a CM5T (4801), a C5 with skylights (4819) in the black and yellow colours of The Lichfield

Speedway Supporters Club and a standard C5 (4780). None was without fault. Both 4780 and 4801 had the non-simplified logo on the boot. This was due to the fact that, at the time, I could only find a rear-view picture of 4774 which showed the logo with oval and wings. 4780 also gained an erroneous window frame within the top glazing of the passenger door. In planning ahead, a moulding for an alternative passenger door had been prepared, so that in the future, a C5A bus could be modelled. Somehow this door found its way on to the yellow and black 4819 which had never been a C5A variant. My favourite followed, CM5T 4807, displaying the white panel on the black roof and twin headlights, although still sporting the wrong logo on the boot. Next came the C5A model, 4833, featuring the appropriate bus door, twin headlights and skylights, with no obvious faults. My least favourite was CM5 4800 on the Coventry motorway service. This had been given a solid silver hub on the rear wheels, instead of the carefully painted red and silver as on other models, and so looked wrong. Also an unwanted additional fog light had crept in, but at least it did have the correct logo on the boot!

It was decided that the special OOC model for 2003[51] should be from the BMMO C5 casting. 4780 was my recommendation, by way of recompense to Andrew Hawthorn for the errors of the first attempt of two years earlier. Andrew was, at that time, the owner of 4780. I proposed that the coach should be modelled as it appeared later in its career and as Andrew hoped to present his restoration, i.e. maroon roof with white panel and skylights. The result was pleasing and the model is probably not so easy to come by. The eighth release formed part of the Midland Red Centenary set of 2004. This consisted of a BMMO D9 and C5A bus

Top: **The Guiterman toy came with an attractive box.**

Above: **The Original Omnibus Company, part of Corgi Classics, released the first three of their C5 castings in April 2001. This photograph shows 4801 and is a most attractive model.**

Below: **An alternative colour scheme for the OOC model is the yellow and black of the Lichfield Speedway Supporters Club coach.**

Notes

51 This was available only to Corgi Collectors Club members who subscribed to the OOC magazine Bus Route.

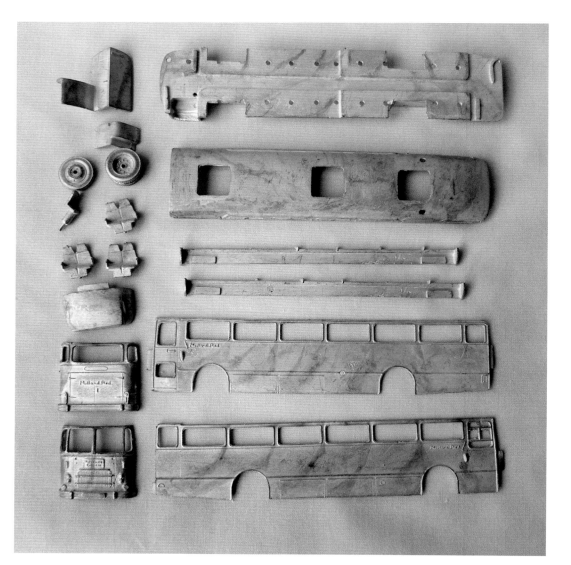

The CM6T motorway coach appeared as a white metal kit in 1992, when it was released by Lowland Model Buses.

A completed Lowland model of the CM6T, built by Roy Finney.

4826. The latter had the destination 'Wythall', by way of a 'thank you' for the help extended to me by the Transport Museum, Wythall over the preceding years when gathering reference material for the OOC Midland Red models. The most recent model is CM5 4833, a Worcester-based motorway coach. There was one minor error which I'll leave the eagle-eyed to spot!

The CM6T did not enjoy the same attention from the toy or model manufacturers. A white metal kit was made by Lowland Model Buses in 1992. It came with alternative parts for both original and restyled versions of the CM6T. In 1997, Pirate Models reissued the kit. This time it came as the original 1965 CM6T (ref 4006) and, as a separate kit, the 1972 restyled version (ref 4108).

In 1998, a 1/50th scale model CM6T was produced by Wheels Model Railways of Nuneaton. Costing £140 each, they were made in polymer resin and hand-painted. A limited run of 500 pieces was produced. This was to pave the way for further models under the banner 'The Midland Red Collection'.

This publicity shot was used to promote the Wheels 1/50th scale resin model of the CM6T.

Finally, the largest of all miniatures was that built by Midland Red's official model builder, Joe Faulkner. Having spent 36 years with the company, he retired in 1960, but not before he had built a 1/12th scale model of the CM5T coach. This was later presented to General Manager, Donald Sinclair, on the occasion of his retirement in 1966. A recognition indeed, that this coach represented the zenith of Sinclair's years at the head of Midland Red.

Standing alongside the real thing is this 1/12th scale CM5T, built by Midland Red's in-house model builder, Joe Faulkner. The model was presented to General Manager, Donald Sinclair, when he retired at the end of 1966. The original Corgi version is dwarfed by comparison. BMMO

CORGI'S ORIGINAL OMNIBUS COMPANY MODELS

Stock code	Variant		Fleet No.	Reg. No.	Destination	Release date	Pieces Made
OM45501	CM5T	BIRMINGHAM-LONDON MOTORWAY EXPRESS	4801	801 HHA	London	Apr-01	8600
OM45502	C5	Lichfield Speedway Supporters Club	-	819 HHA	-	Apr-01	5000
OM45503	C5	Standard Coach	4780	780 GHA	Llandudno	Apr-01	5000
OM45504	CM5T	BIRMINGHAM-LONDON MOTORWAY EXPRESS	4807	807 HHA	Birmingham	Aug-01	2900
OM45505	C5A	Midland Red Bus Route 789	4833	833 HHA	Tamworth	Jun-01	4000
OM45506	CM5	COVENTRY-LONDON MOTORWAY EXPRESS	4800	800 HHA	London	Jan-03	2200
OM45507	C5	Standard Coach	4780	780 GHA	New Brighton	Apr-03	1000
OM45508A	CM5	BIRMINGHAM-SELLY OAK-WORCESTER EXPRESS	4833	833 HHA	Birmingham	Jun-09	750
OM45508B	CM5	BIRMINGHAM-SELLY OAK-WORCESTER EXPRESS	4833	833 HHA	Worcester	Jun-09	750
Midland Red Centenary Gift Set							
OM99146	C5A	Midland Red Bus Route 172	4826	826 HHA	Wythall	Mar-04	2600

DIGBETH AND VICTORIA COACH STATIONS

Digbeth

In July 1925, BMMO acquired a substantial site to the west of Digbeth's High Street, with Mill Lane at the northern end and Rea Street to the south. This was an ideal location for a city centre bus garage and coach station which, following demolition of existing buildings, was built and completed by the start of January 1929.

This was by far the company's biggest depot and incorporated their premier coach station, used by its own vehicles and those from associated companies. Midland Red was a founder member of Associated Motorways, which was formed in 1934. The association's purpose was to pool members' services between the Midlands, the south and west of England and between London and South Wales. Each member company committed itself to providing an agreed mileage of coach journeys for Associated Motorways, then taking an agreed share of the profits.

After war commenced in September 1939, the coach station element of Digbeth would have near-mirrored the passenger trends being experienced at Victoria Coach Station (*see later*). However, unlike Victoria, the site at Digbeth was a major garage and so was kept fully occupied. Near disaster struck when, in

March 1944, a Wellington bomber crashed on to Mill Lane, but the only Midland Red property damaged was one double-decker bus.

Following the conversion of the main road to dual carriageway in the early 1950s, BMMO was in a position to acquire land and construct a much improved frontage to the garage. This opened in June 1958, and the new facilities were a boon to the coach station. Included in the long frontage, which was four storeys high, was a booking hall, enquiry area, left luggage and lost property facilities, toilets, extensive seating accommodation for waiting passengers, as well as a 100-seat self-service restaurant.

So it was that, when the motorway service opened nearly 18 months later, the facilities were fit for purpose. Coaches had long entered into the station from Rea Street through one of three gateways and certainly by the time of the motorway service, four lanes were used, each with a number of stands running most of the length of the building. Refuelling points were at the entrance gateways and once Midland Red vehicles were unloaded, drivers were required to go around the block to refuel, prior to finishing their duty.

In the 1970s, alterations were made. These included dispensing with the bus maintenance pits and increasing the coach lanes to

Below: An excellent photograph taken inside Digbeth Coach Station, circa 1960, showing a line of three CM5Ts, headed by 4802. Chris Hodge Trucks Neg no. aaa616

Opposite page:

CM5T 4805 heads south on the dual carriageway with Digbeth Coach Station on the left. Chris Hodge Trucks Neg no. aaa631

Digbeth Coach Station was also a bus garage and this photograph bears witness to the dual role. The double-decker near the entrance, is a Leyland PD2 BMMO type designation LD8. G H F Atkins/© and courtesy John Banks Collection

five. The exit was changed from the three doorways to one large one. Over the ensuing years the coach station became somewhat dingy and was not becoming for the nation's second city. The premises, having long been owned by National Express, closed on 12th November 2008, to be demolished and entirely rebuilt. In the meanwhile, a temporary coach station was opened opposite. The new Birmingham Coach Station opened for business on 14th December 2009, having cost £15 million.

Victoria

London Victoria Coach Station, located in Buckingham Palace Road, was owned and administered by London Coastal Coaches Limited, an association of coach operators, like Associated Motorways already referred to. It was built on a three-acre site and opened in 1932. The Art Deco style building was designed by architects Wallis, Gilbert and Partners. The frontage was given an impressive clock tower and upon entering, to the left was the main passenger waiting area, whilst going to the right led on to the concourse which consisted of the numbered stands and passenger queuing areas. Facing them were the coach bays in

which the coaches waited line astern. The lead coach pulled forward to load. Once the coach was in position, the passengers would cross the exit lane to board. Stands and loading were protected by a cantilever glass canopy. Vehicles left the coach station via Elizabeth Street, while entry was from Semley Place.

After war was declared in 1939, the coach station experienced a big increase in traffic. This was due to operators transporting anxious parents from London to various parts of the country in order to visit their evacuated children. This was to be short-lived as fuel rationing and vehicle shortages restricted travel. By mid-1942 London Coastal found a quarter of its London agencies had closed and by September of that year, the ministry responsible for war transport suspended the operation of most express services, leaving the station virtually inactive. During the following years the US Army used part of the station as a vehicle-repair depot. Apart from losing the glass of the roof canopy, the coach station survived the blitz.

In March 1946, services were restarted and the full range of Associated Motorways routes was operational by June. Fuel rationing ceased at the close of 1948, bringing a return to near normal activity.

Midland Red vehicles were regular visitors using this terminus for their long-distance coach routes as well as for private hire work, although the latter required prior arrangement. It was when the motorway service opened in November 1959, that many more Birmingham people would make use of this convenient facility.

Located on the opposite side of Elizabeth Street was the garage of coach operator Samuelsons. This was used as a repair and refuelling base for coaches on express services as well Samuelsons' own stock and also, from the 1970s, as an unloading station. This facility provided a limited back-up for Midland Red. A small number of their mechanics had received basic instruction relating to the differences in BMMO coaches from other more familiar makes. Accordingly, a few custom spares were held in stock.

In 1970, Victoria Coach Station became the responsibility of the NBC subsidiary, National Travel (South East) Limited. In 1978, London Coastal Coaches Company was reborn and they formed Victoria Coach Station Limited. In 1988, following the privatisation of the NBC companies, ownership of Victoria Coach Station Limited was transferred to London Transport.

Between 1990 and 1994, major works were carried out costing over £4.8 million. In 2000, ownership passed to Transport for London who, in 2008, carried out modest building work at a cost of £320,000.

Victoria Coach Station was built to an art deco style in 1932. This photograph was taken on 2nd November 1999, when C5 4819 celebrated the 40th anniversary of the motorway express service.
Nick Larkin

Top left: **Prototype C5, 4722, on a visit to Victoria Coach Station in March 1965.** Ken Jubb

Top right: **Probably taken in the late 1960s, this picture shows CM6T 5649 at Victoria Coach Station waiting to head back to Digbeth.** BaMMOT

Centre: **Samuelsons depot was situated on the other side of Elizabeth Street, opposite Victoria Coach Station. The facility provided limited technical back-up for Midland Red coaches and was later also used as an unloading area.** G H F Atkins/© and courtesy John Banks Collection

Bottom: **Standing under the cantilever canopy at Victoria Coach Station in August 1972, is CM6T 5652. This vehicle was the first to appear in the NBC white livery. The route number MM1 is unusual.** T W Moore

D. M. SINCLAIR

Donald McIntyre Sinclair was General Manager of the Birmingham and Midland Motor Omnibus Company Ltd for all of its most illustrious years (1944-1966). He was born 18th December 1901, in Glasgow and received a good education culminating in studies at the city's Royal Technical College. There was a likelihood that he would enter the ship-building industry but instead, he became an apprentice with the Scotland-based Albion Motor Car Co Ltd.

His next job was with a Perthshire bus company where, as well as being a maintenance engineer, he did spells as both a bus driver and a conductor. Next, he moved into car repair work. Things settled down when, in 1924, he joined British Petroleum Co Ltd as assistant branch engineer in charge of transport, first working at Bedford and Croydon and then, a year later, as branch engineer at Bristol.

In 1931, Donald Sinclair made the move which would shape the rest of his working life. He joined Northern General Transport Co Ltd at Gateshead, becoming assistant to Gordon Hayter, the Chief Engineer. 'Northern General', as it was known, was a part of the British Electric Traction group which also included Midland Red.

Here, Sinclair was exposed to BMMO-built SOS chassis, together with their single-deck bodies of BMMO design; Northern General ran more than 200 of these vehicles.

Northern General was impressed with AEC's Q series of side-engined buses which were in use with London Transport.[52] This

Donald McIntyre Sinclair was 'Mr Midland Red' from 1944 until his retirement on the last day of 1966.

On display in the Power Hall at the Transport Museum, Wythall, is this surviving example of a Northern General SOS Q single-deck bus. Author

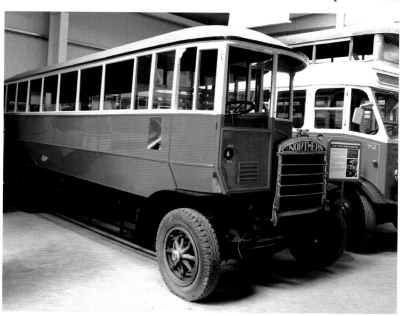

layout offered additional passenger seating without infringement of the maximum bus dimensions then in force. As a result Northern General developed and built side-engined buses for their own use following BMMO's lead in home built vehicles; Sinclair was at the heart of things.

When Midland Red's Chief Engineer, L.G. Wyndham Shire, retired, Donald Sinclair filled the vacancy arriving at the company in May 1940. His appointment was of great significance, firstly to Midland Red and in no small measure to the bus industry as a whole. In that same month Winston Churchill was fulfilling his own destiny, as he took over the reins of government at the nation's hour of need.

Sinclair made an early mark by replacing the 'SOS' radiator badge on the company's buses (Shire's Own Specification?), with the company monogram 'BMMO'. At a time when bus production was grinding to a halt, in order that all possible resources could be given over to war work, the new Chief Engineer had his sights on new, even revolutionary designs. He took the four experimental rear-engined vehicles developed by his predecessor and proceeded to investigate the underfloor engine concept. Presumably he side-stepped bans on building new buses as he was 'rebuilding' existing ones. Not only was his eye on the mechanical aspect of vehicles but also their appearance. He gave a stylish front end to a pre-war FEDD type double-decker, which concealed the front wing, radiator and bonnet in an all-encompassing bonnet and grille. He registered this style as a BMMO design in January 1943 and when a decade later the company took deliv-

Notes

52 When the first AEC Q single-decker was delivered into service in September 1932 the fleet name was still the London General Omnibus Company.

53 Until this point, the company had been jointly managed by the Chief Engineer and Traffic Manager.

When it appeared in 1944, the D1 bus, of which there was just the one example, reflected Sinclair's thinking about bus body styling. It spent virtually all of its working life operating from Bearwood garage. Alan D Broughall

ery of 100 Leyland PD2s, BMMO stipulated this type of front end to fit in with the rest of the fleet. Other Leyland customers requested the same design which was referred to as the 'BMMO front'.

As soon as building restrictions were eased a little in 1944, Sinclair built a brand new prototype double-decker, the D1. In 1946, the production version of the wartime underfloor-engined single-deck buses appeared. This was the S6, and like the D1 had an attractive modern body. These soon started to enter service as did double-deckers, based on the D1, before the decade was out. Other bus manufacturers were years behind on a comparable vehicle to the S6 and the delay in getting the new-look double-decker into service was simply due to lack of building capacity, both on the part of BMMO and outside body builders. This

leap forward, in both mechanical and styling designs, would continue to mark Donald Sinclair's years at the helm.

Back to 1944, Midland Red's Traffic Manager, O.C. Power, died suddenly in office and it was Donald Sinclair who stepped into the breach by becoming General Manager whilst continuing as Chief Engineer.[53] Midland Red was the largest bus undertaking outside of London Transport and Sinclair had proved his worth during the preceding war years, overseeing a large fleet of buses under the most adverse of conditions, yet had still been able to give his mind to experimental and development work. In January 1946, he passed the title of Chief Engineer to S.C. Vince, whilst he kept overall control as General Manager.

Still in 1946, he built the experimental integral S5, which was the forerunner of the

The use of fibreglass in the construction of bus bodies was a typical innovation of Midland Red under the leadership of Donald Sinclair. These two photographs show the one-piece roof of an S14 being fitted. BMMO

An amusing cartoon from 'Frostie' celebrating Donald Sinclair driving the CM5 coach.

A major building project during Donald Sinclair's years at Midland Red was the expansion of the Central Works at Edgbaston. This aerial view was taken in 1969. BMMO

unique S14. This first put in an appearance in 1953, with its other innovative features such as disc brakes, rubber suspension and the use of fibreglass. And so the cutting edge designs kept on coming. The year 1958 brought the unveiling of the superb-looking and highly-advanced 72-seat D9 and, of course, in the same year the decision was made to apply for a licence to run the motorway express service. The following year saw the development and introduction into service of the ground-breaking CM5T. Sinclair's belief for some 20 years in the underfloor-engine concept culminated in two experimental double-deckers using this layout. Known as the D10, the type didn't go into production but the two buses put in years of service at Stafford. The second generation of motorway coach was again more than a match for anything else on the road and deliveries of these were completed by the time D.M. Sinclair retired on 31st December 1966, aged 65.

Not only was Sinclair 'hands on' in all of the above, but he also oversaw many building projects, notable among which was the expansion of Central Works, Edgbaston (completed in 1954) and Digbeth Coach

A major project for Midland Red was the building of the Bull Ring Bus Station. This photograph was taken in 1971 and features BMMO D9 4942 (942 KHA). Author

Station (opened in 1958) as well as the building of the Bull Ring Bus Station (opened in 1963).

Donald Sinclair also became Chairman of Black and White Motorways of Cheltenham, and a Director of Stratford-upon-Avon Blue Motors, The Warwick and Leamington Transport Co Ltd and Majestic Express Motors Ltd. As an engineer he was a Member of the Institution of Mechanical Engineers, as well as the Institute of Transport. He was also a council member of the Public Transport Association and gained Fellowship of the Institute of Directors. He was recognised in the 1950 New Years Honours, being awarded the CBE. He became President of the Omnibus Society in 1953.

Donald Sinclair married Catherine MacGregor and had three daughters Margaret, Patricia and Catherine, and a number of grandchildren. He was polite but remained somewhat aloof from those further down the chain; some said dour. He apparently found time to engage in fishing, shooting and golf. As often seemed the case in those days, he only saw a few years of retirement, dying on 17th June 1971.

Donald Sinclair with a variety of Midland Red models, built by resident model-maker, Joe Faulkner. BMMO

THE MIRA PROVING GROUND

This page:

The MIRA circuit proved invaluable when testing the CM5 prototype. The coach is seen here in early Spring 1959.
Photo via Jim Pearson

Opposite page:

Top: **Jim Pearson is at the wheel of the CM5 prototype as it travels on the lower-speed circuit at MIRA.** Photo via Jim Pearson

Bottom left: **The famous publicity picture of CM5T 4801 on the high-speed circuit. Ken Worrall is behind the wheel, with fellow Technical Assistant, Trevor Yeo, to his left.**
BMMO

Bottom right: **This cartoon appeared in the Midland Red staff** *Bulletin*.

BMMO was a member of the Motor Industry Research Association. From as early as 1950, the company used the association's proving ground which is located near Nuneaton. Structural integrity tests were conducted over the Belgian pavé and for ride quality over the corrugated surface. Other facilities used included the turning circle, a circuit for brake fade tests and water-splash. It was, however, the testing of the motorway coaches which brought home just how valuable the proving ground was, especially the high-speed circuit. As Jim Pearson, the Development Engineer for BMMO, points out, 'How else could we have done the testing? We could hardly have gone over to Germany to use the autobahns nor could we simply use the Preston by-pass. MIRA was also very co-operative when it came to using the high-speed circuit for instructing the first motorway coach drivers.' Jim says that to the best of his recollection, following the opening of the high-speed circuit, access to the facility was under the circuit through a tunnel. 'This had quite a dip and we could just get the S14 through without catching the roof and I don't think we risked the CM5. Because of the dip we always took single-decks over 30 feet in length and of course double-deckers via the overhead route using a short section of the high speed circuit. This was only done after receiving clearance from the control tower.'

The high-speed circuit had been opened in May 1954, following closely the perimeter track of the former airfield on which the proving ground was built. The circuit of 2.8 miles consisted of a track which was divided into two lanes, separated by a white line. The maximum permitted speed on the inside track and the minimum on the outside was 70 mph. Overtaking was allowed, although restricted to the straights on the outer lane. The lanes were of equal width on the straights but, because of a greater amount of lower-speed traffic, the inner lane was wider than the outer on the bends. The number of vehicles using the circuit at any one time was restricted, ten on the inner lane and five on the faster, outer lane. If a vehicle on the outer lane was exceeding 100 mph, then only two other vehicles were permitted to share it. Traffic was monitored from the control tower and clearance had to be obtained before switching to the outer lane. Banking was a feature of the high-speed circuit, this being in three places. When the CM5 prototype was taken on to the outer lane, it was the first heavy vehicle officially allowed on.

"That was Stirling Moss we just passed!"

The Proving Ground

The Motor Industry Research Association was formed in 1946, but its history can be traced back some 40 years earlier. In 1906, the Cycle Engineers' Institute became the Incorporated Institution of Automobile Engineers (later rebranded as IAE). Following the First World War, in 1919 the Joint Technical Committee was formed between the IAE and the Society of Motor Manufacturers and Traders (SMMT) with the brief to '... co-operate in all the technical matters connected with the automobile and kindred industries'. The Research branch of the Association of British Motor and Allied Manufacturers (RABMAM) evolved from this Joint Technical Committee. RABMAM developed into the Auto Research Committee (ARC). Later in 1946, while the IAE became the Automobile Division of the Institute of Mechanical Engineers, MIRA was born from ARC.

After the Second World War, the nation's export effort was an essential element in getting the country back on its feet. Export of motor vehicles, which before the war had been of secondary importance, was now key.

Upon the formation of MIRA, its management saw the need for a proving ground where British-built vehicles could be 'proved' in the type of road conditions that they would meet overseas. These, for the most part, were far less developed than in Britain. Whilst this was certainly so for the 'territories', as the nations of the British Empire were known, it was also true of the many bumpy or pavé road surfaces on the European continent.

MIRA recommended building a proving ground with the General Motors, Michigan establishment as a model. The emphasis for such a construction would be to perfectly simulate the rough road surfaces and conditions which British-made vehicles would encounter overseas. These severe yet controlled conditions would be of a permanent nature enabling manufacturers to return months, even years later, safe in the knowledge that consistent formulation of data could be obtained. Also recognised was the need to study, in a systematic way, various performance characteristics. The need to provide and develop accelerated endurance testing was a requirement from the outset.

At first, the idea for the proving ground was given a lukewarm reception, not by engineers within the British motor industry, who were keen, but from those at management level. Their concern was twofold. Firstly, the amount of finance which would be needed to establish and then maintain such a facility was well in excess of anything attempted previously by such a co-operative of interested parties. Secondly, hitherto much secrecy had accompanied individual members' research and development work. A proving ground was perceived as an 'open house' for competitors to view one another's efforts.

Nevertheless, a determined case was made by a core group within MIRA, headed by Dr. Albert Fogg. Some initial finance appears to have been raised by obtaining Government grants, which at that time were available to the motor industry as part of the export drive. The intention was that a proving ground would be built and then developed over time. The issue of concerns about secrecy was soon to be seen as something of a red herring.

Where to site such a large establishment – it would need to be at least one square mile – was another hurdle to be overcome. One of the then-disused wartime airfields was an obvious choice, but it would need to be geographically convenient to the majority of motor industry companies which were members of the association. After the surveying of 15 such airfields, former RAF Nuneaton in Leicestershire[54] was selected as best. The proving ground would occupy 760 acres.

This RAF airfield had opened in February 1943 as a satellite to RAF Bramcote. Unlike Bramcote, RAF Nuneaton (also known as both Lindley and Lindley Lodge) had concrete runways rather than Bramcote's grass with steel matting. It was home to 105 Operational Training Unit (OTU) which used elderly Wellington 1c[55] aircraft. The perimeter track, runways and even the control tower formed a foundation for the planned facilities.

Ossie Dolby, a former Major in the REME who had served in the Far East during the war, was appointed superintendent of the proving ground. He was the first full-time

This aerial view of RAF Nuneaton, taken in August 1945, shows the perimeter track and runway layout. At least 33 Wellington aircraft are visible on the original print.
Photo via Dick Nutt

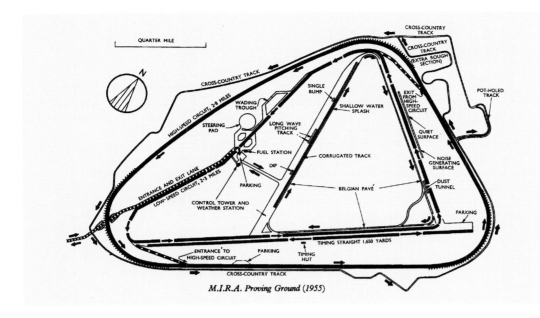

M.I.R.A. Proving Ground (1955)

Notes

54 The town of Nuneaton is located in the county of Warwickshire, whilst the former airfield, RAF Nuneaton, falls within the county of Leicestershire.

55 By way of an interesting digression, a Wellington (serial number HD987) was flying a night exercise from RAF Nuneaton on 22nd March 1944. It reported an engine failure before crashing on to Mill Lane, Digbeth, Birmingham. It narrowly missed the Midland Red garage, but did damage a company double-decker. All three crew were killed...

employee of the new facility, joining the operation in the summer of 1948. Although the job title changed, Ossie Dolby remained in post until his retirement in 1980, running the site along military lines. The industry started to use the proving ground in October of that year, although the test tracks only consisted of the disused runways. The banked high-speed circuit was opened in May 1954. A study of the accompanying site plan shows the range of facilities available in 1955.

During the 1950s and 1960s, the services and facilities of MIRA were being built up. For many years Government grants and members' funding was provided to allow the Motor Industry Research Association to fulfil its calling, *viz* fundamental research, deemed necessary for the industry it served. However, over the years MIRA was also carrying out private tests, these being for the benefit of specific members, rather than for the industry as a whole. Later, as the amount of private testing increased, a scale of charging was introduced. Throughout the 1960s these quasi-commercial activities increased and gave MIRA experience in contract work. From 1958, members were expressing the desire that they wanted continued research programmes, but with increased private test work in order to meet their short-term needs.

Another source of income generated by the MIRA Proving Ground resulted from farming. Part of the lease requirement, imposed by the Air Ministry, was that land not used for automotive testing should be farmed. In the early days, this involved sub-tenants who were already in residence, but following an accident, MIRA itself assumed full responsibility employing their own farmer, Mr Trevor Colgate, who stayed until about 1955. After this time the farming work became the responsibility of MIRA's superintendent, Ossie Dolby.

The farming aspect included the growing of broad beans and grain, but when markets fluctuated diversification saw the introduction of pig-farming. In the early days the farming activities yielded a profit of around £500 per annum and by 1980 this had increased to about £30,000 per annum. With the demands of the (then) European Economic Community (EEC) Common Agricultural Policy and other 'red tape', MIRA decided to concentrate solely on its automotive activities and ceased farming.

Since 1975, the funding arrangements for belonging to the organisation went from a membership subscription for car companies to a fee-based system. On 4th July 2001, the organisation changed its name to MIRA Ltd. Currently, the site has test equipment valued in excess of £100 million and, 60 years on, is very much in business.

This aerial view shows the MIRA Proving Ground as it was in 1965. Significant extensions have taken place in the ten years since the plan above.
Photo via Dick Nutt

HEADING FOR THE MOTORWAYS

British troops in Germany, during the immediate post-war years, were impressed when they saw, and drove on, the autobahns. These fast roads, with their flyovers and large blue and white signage (shades of things to come in Britain), had been built between 1932 and 1942. During that period, Germany had constructed 2,000 miles of dual carriageway; the first autobahn actually opened as early as 1929. Italy too had developed its autostrada network, commencing in 1924. It is not surprising therefore, that after the Second World War, the Ministry of Transport published a paper which showed that 10% of Britain's roads were carrying 60% of the traffic. The Ministry concluded that a comparatively small mileage of new high-quality roads, which were unimpeded by cross-traffic or obstruction, the cause of bunching, would result in a great improvement to traffic flow. Such new road-building would include dual carriageways together with motorways.

In 1946, a tentative plan for road-building, which included provision for 800 miles of motorways, was published by the Ministry of Transport. However, due to the economic climate of the immediate post-war years the plans were put on hold. Up until this time, British roads were legally available to all traffic: pedestrians, pedal cycles, horses etc. This would need to change for the proposed motorways, and in 1949 'The Special Roads Act' was passed. This Act allowed for the Ministry or Local Authority to specify the types of traffic permitted on to a given road scheme.

In 1951, consulting engineers, Sir Owen Williams and Partners, were asked to carry out a preliminary survey as to the practicability of building a motorway from the proposed St Albans by-pass, northwards to Doncaster. In February 1955, the Minister of Transport announced plans to build not only the London-to-Yorkshire motorway, but also the Birmingham-to-Preston and the Ross Spur motorways.

As a result, the Preston by-pass, the first instalment of what would become the M6 Motorway, was started in 1956. It was opened by the Prime Minister, Harold Macmillan, on 5th December 1958, and so was the first length of motorway in Britain, although it was never allocated an 'M' title in its own right.

M1 Motorway

The first major project, that of the London-to-Birmingham Motorway, which was actually the first part of the London-to-Yorkshire M1 Motorway, commenced on 24th March 1958. This would include a southern spur, the M10, and a northern spur, the M45.[56] Despite its name (the London-to-Birmingham Motorway), in reality the project actually stopped short of Birmingham by some 28 miles!

This first section of the M1 building project was an unprecedented achievement taking, as it did, just 586 days to construct 72 miles of road with its accompanying 183 bridges. This worked out at an average of one mile of dual carriageway every eight days and one bridge every three days. It was completed on time and within its £16.5 million budget.

Much of the traffic on the new motorway would be taken from the London-to-Holyhead road (A5), Weedon-to-Birmingham road (A45) and to a lesser extent the London-to-Birmingham road (A41). Initial estimates were that 14,000 vehicles a day would use the M1.

MOTORWAY DESCRIPTION IN BRIEF	
Formation Width M1	112ft
Formation Width M45 and M10	88ft
Carriageway width M1 (3 lanes in each direction)	36ft
Carriageway width M45 and M10 (2 lanes in each direction)	24ft
Maximum gradient	1 in 30
Horizontal curvature minimum radius	2,864ft
Grassed central reservation width generally	15ft
Reinforced hard shoulder width	8ft
White marginal strips to mark the edges of the carriageway	
White lane markings with reflective studs (catseyes)	

Five million tons of building material, including stone, sand, cement and steel, were taken on to the road, to form the foundation, surface and bridge works. Twenty million tons of earth, gravel rock and chalk were redistributed as heights were lowered and dips filled. This cut-and-fill made economic sense and embankments were generally kept below 25ft, although in places this did reach 40ft.

The Chief Engineer at the Ministry of Transport, J. F. A. Baker, was in overall charge of this massive project. Sir Owen Williams and Partners who, as mentioned above, did the initial survey work, designed and supervised the biggest section, that of the 55 miles north of St. Albans (incorporating the northern spur); the work being done by John Laing and Son Ltd. Tarmac Civil Engineering had the contract for the next 12 miles south (incorporating the southern spur). This section had a concrete surface, the first time this was used on motorway construction in Britain; asphalt was the norm.

The Dunchurch by-pass was built as part of the main John Laing contract. Here C5 4819 is seen using the road on the occasion of the 40th anniversary commemorative run.
Author

A consortium of companies built the remaining five miles – the Watford by-pass. Amazingly, only five houses and three bungalows were demolished to make way for the motorway.

The motorway was opened with a small ceremony by the Minister of Transport, Ernest Marples, at 9:30 am on 2nd November 1959, at Slip End, Toddington[57] in Bedfordshire. The Minister said that the road was '…in keeping with the bold, exciting and scientific age in which we live.' Yet a few hours later, at a commemorative luncheon being held at London's Savoy Hotel, he expressed his shock and horror at the behaviour of the first drivers using the motorway. 'I was frightened when I saw the first drivers using the road. I'd never seen anybody going so fast and ignoring the rules and regulations. Of the first four cars I saw, three[58] were not keeping to their traffic lanes; they were straddling them. Another car came along and broke down!'

At the head of the queue to get on the M45 Motorway near Dunchurch was a Ford Consul carrying the Walsh family from Birmingham; motoring journalists were equally keen to get on the motorway. They relished the new experience, reporting on driving at over 100 mph in their sports cars on a pristine road. A total of 3,000 vehicles used the motorway in the first hour. The first Sunday after opening saw this figure peak at 5,000 an hour, as a Sunday afternoon drive took on a new meaning. The motorway became a popular destination for drivers, as well as passive observers of the new road. Indeed, London Transport was soon laying on scores of Sunday services, just to take people to see the motorway.

Marples' fears were expressions of concern long held by civil servants and journalists. Would the nation's drivers and vehicles be able to cope with the conditions and speeds of the new motorway? Much effort was expended by

Notes

56 Also built as part of the northern spur was the three-mile long Dunchurch by-pass.

57 Toddington would become Granada's first motorway service area, opening in 1965.

58 A Rover, Bentley and Jaguar.

CM6T 5648 travels along the M45 Motorway with a full load bound for London in 1966. T W Moore

Although taken from a vantage point which is now within the M25 orbital motorway, this photograph, taken circa 1960, shows just how free of traffic the M1 Motorway was at that time. The CM5T heading for London is 4802. Arthur Hustwitt © NA3T

motoring organisations, police and civil servants in order to minimise bad driving practice. As anticipated, many vehicles did prove inadequate to the task of extended periods of high-speed motoring. Drivers were tempted by the unrestricted speed permitted, but it was only the Jaguars, Bentleys, a few sports cars and the Midland Red motorway coaches which proved equal to the job. For the first few weeks, the press seemed to delight in reporting statistics about crashes and fatalities. Matters were not helped by the bad weather conditions of that first winter.

Nevertheless, once the dust settled, people welcomed the motorway. It offered freedom and was seen as a promise of a new and exciting Britain, the Britain of the 1960s. On 15th August 1960 the service area at Newport Pagnell (operated by Fortes) opened.[59] It became a destination in its own right for many people (especially young adults).

Other Motorways...

Other motorways relevant to this particular book are: the Ross Spur (M50), the first section of the M5 and later sections of the M6.

The Ross Spur was a useful training ground for Midland Red's Worcester drivers, who had been chosen to operate the X44 route, using CM5 coaches. Building of this two-lane motorway started in March 1958 and would initially run between the A38 near Tewkesbury to just beyond Ross-on-Wye, a length of 20 miles. Dimensions were to the standard of the day for motorway construction, the surface being asphalt. The project was shared between three contractors and involved the building of 39 bridges. It is reckoned that this was the least expensive motorway ever built, costing just £6 million and opened in November 1960.

A far bigger project, surprisingly of two-lane design also, was the M5. This would eventually connect the industrial West Midlands with the South West. The first length was from the M50 northwards to Lydiate Ash, which is two miles to the south of Rubery, on the outskirts of Birmingham.

This 28½ mile length of motorway was built by A. Monk Co Ltd. Work commenced in April 1960 and was scheduled for completion by October 1961. Subsequently, this was put back to 20th July 1962. Included within the project was the extension of the M50, from the A38 junction to join the M5 at Strensham.

Whilst the lane width was the same as that of earlier motorways, the central reservation was two feet narrower, but the hard shoulder width was increased by one foot. The surface of the main carriageways was asphalt.

In November 1965, the M5 was extended northwards by six miles, reaching the Hagley Road at Quinton. This new section enabled Midland Red to start the X43 Birmingham-Worcester service which routed via Bearwood. It was not until May 1970 that the 9-mile link, from Quinton to the M6, was opened.

The M6, which would eventually connect the M1 in Leicestershire with Carlisle in the North, was built in isolated sections which were gradually linked. Midland Red was able to use the joined-up motorway to operate its ME3 Coventry-Birmingham-Glasgow service from the late 1960s. The section of M6, linking Gravelly Hill with the M1, was fully opened by November 1971. In turn, Birmingham's city centre was linked with the Gravelly Hill interchange (Spaghetti Junction) by the A38(M) Aston Expressway. This innovative piece of road, with its variable lane[60] directions designed to accommodate rush-hour traffic, opened in May 1972. For Midland Red coach drivers leaving Digbeth Coach Station needing to access the M1 and M6 Motorways, this became the preferred route.

Notes

59 Initially, this service area was for cars only. Watford Gap service area (operated by Blue Boar) had opened on the day the M1 Motorway opened and was for lorries only. However, buildings were incomplete and food and drink were served from brightly painted temporary wooden sheds.

60 Formally known as 'tidal flow' to allow better management of traffic. Lane use is controlled by means of electronic overhead signs, with one lane always closed to create a buffer between the two directions of travel – there is no central reservation. In the morning, four of the seven lanes are designated for use by traffic heading toward Birmingham city centre, and two lanes for traffic out of the city. In the evening rush hour, this pattern is reversed and four lanes are made available to outbound traffic and two lanes towards the city centre. At all other times, the road runs with three lanes in each direction. (See http://en.wikipedia.org/wiki/A38(M)_motorway#Tidal_flow)

Life in the fast lane. CM5 4812 returns to Coventry with Newport Pagnell services in the background. The picture was taken either in late 1960 or 1961. 4812 was the first of the C5 class to be withdrawn following a serious accident in June 1967. BMMO

Not Bertie the Bus v Thomas the Tank Engine but CM6T 5295 and E3049, a class AL2 (later class 82) locomotive, near Newport Pagnell some time between 1965-1967. BMMO

VEHICLE HISTORIES and GARAGE ALLOCATIONS

PRODUCTION SCHEDULE C5/CM5/CM5T

Type	Year Built	Registration Number	Fleet Number
BMMO C5 (prototype)	1958	722 BHA	4722
BMMO C5	1958	774-76 GHA, 799 GHA, 778 GHA	4774-76, 4777, 4778
BMMO C5	1959	779-95 GHA	4779-95
BMMO C5	1960	796-98 GHA, 799 HHA	4796-98, 4799
BMMO C5	1961	816-25, 827-29, 831-37 HHA	4816-25, 4827-29, 4831-37
BMMO CM5	1959	805-08 HHA	4805-08
BMMO CM5	1960	800, 812/13 HHA	4800, 4812/13
BMMO CM5T	1959	801-04, 809/10 HHA	4801-04, 4809/10
BMMO CM5T	1960	811, 814/15 HHA	4811, 4814/15
BMMO CM5T	1961	826 HHA, 830 HHA	4826, 4830

Total 65

PRODUCTION SCHEDULE CM6/CM6T

Type	Year Built	Registration Number	Fleet Number
BMMO CM6T (prototype)	1963	5495 HA	5295
BMMO CM6T	1965	BHA 646-59C	5646-59
BMMO CM6T	1965	DHA 960-65C	5660-65
BMMO CM6T	1966	EHA 666/72-74D	5666/72-74
BMMO CM6	1966	EHA 667-71D	5667-71

Total 30

BODY TYPE AND SEATING CONFIGURATION DECODE

C5 and CM5	C37F	CM5T	C34F
CM6	C46F	CM6T	C44F

C = Coach;   34, 37, 44 and 46 = Seating Capacity;   F = Front Entrance;   M = Motorway;   T = Toilet

MODIFICATIONS

CS5   =   C37F   5-speed gearbox, non-turbocharged 'KL' engine but with increased fuel injector pressure, 10x20 in. front tyres and stiffened suspension.

C5A   =   C37F   Any variant converted to bus duties (with or without one-man-operation equipment).

4805-07 converted to CM5T (C34F) 1959-60.

4803 converted to C5 (C37F) 1961.

4777, 4779, 4822-23/31-37 converted to CM5 (C37F) 1962-63.

4774/77/79/84-86/94-96, 4801-02/05-06/11/22-23/26/37 converted to CS5 1961-63, C37F except 4806/11, C34F.

Between December 1965 and July 1969 4774-79/81/83/87-90/92/94/98, 4800-15/17-18/20-21/23/26/28-29/31-36 converted to C5A (C37F). Thus the only vehicles to retain their original role were 4780/82/91/93/97/99, 4816/19/24/25/27 all C5s and 4830 a CM5T.

5295 Delivered 03/63 with lantern windscreen and C46FT but by the end of the year had a flat windscreen and C44FT layout.

5654 converted to CM6A 1971 and then to CM6 1972.

5648/50-53/56-58/60-66/68/70/74 went through the restyling programme 1972-73.

INDIVIDUAL VEHICLE GARAGE ALLOCATIONS & SERVICE HISTORY*

MIDLAND RED GARAGE CODES

Only properties relevant to the C5 and CM6 class and sub-classes are listed. County names are as at the period covered i.e. 1958-74 and prior to the formation of the West Midlands county.

BD	BEARWOOD	Bearwood Road, Smethwick, Warley, Staffordshire (becoming Worcestershire in 1966).
BE	BROMSGROVE	Birmingham Road, Bromsgrove, Worcestershire.
BY	BANBURY	Canal Street, Banbury, Oxfordshire.
CE	COALVILLE	Ashby Road, Coalville, Leicestershire.
CY†	CRADLEY HEATH	Forge Lane, Cradley Heath, Staffordshire.
DH	BIRMINGHAM	Rea Street, Digbeth, Birmingham.
DY	DUDLEY	Birmingham Road, Dudley, Worcestershire.
EM	EVESHAM	Abbey Road, Evesham, Worcestershire.
HD	HEREFORD	Friar Street, Hereford.
HL	HARTS HILL	Dudley Road, Harts Hill, Brierley Hill, Staffordshire.
HY	HINCKLEY	Coventry Road, Hinckley, Leicestershire.
KR	KIDDERMINSTER	New Road, Kidderminster, Worcestershire.
LD	LICHFIELD	Trent Valley Road, Lichfield, Staffordshire.
LN	LEAMINGTON	Old Warwick Road, Leamington Spa, Warwickshire.
MD	MARKFIELD	Shaw Lane, Markfield, Leicestershire.
MN	MALVERN	Spring Lane, Malvern Link, Worcestershire.
NN	NUNEATON	Coton Road, Nuneaton, Warwickshire (1921-1960).
		Newtown Road, Nuneaton, Warwickshire.
OY	OLDBURY	Birchley Crossing, Wolverhampton New Road, Oldbury, Worcestershire.
RH	REDDITCH	Church Road, Redditch, Worcestershire.
RY	RUGBY	Railway Terrace, Rugby, Warwickshire.
SA	LEICESTER	Sandacre Street, Leicester.
SD	STAFFORD	Pilgrim Place, Newport Road, Stafford.
SE	STOURBRIDGE	Foster Street, Stourbridge, Worcestershire.
SH	BIRMINGHAM	Sheepcote Street, Edgbaston, Birmingham.
SN	SUTTON COLDFIELD	Upper Holland Road, Sutton Coldfield, Warwickshire.
SS	LEICESTER	Southgate Street, Leicester.
SW	SWADLINCOTE	Midland Road, Swadlincote, Derbyshire.
SY	SHREWSBURY	Ditherington Road, Shrewsbury, Shropshire.
TH	TAMWORTH	Aldergate, Tamworth, Staffordshire.
WL	WELLINGTON	Charlton Street, Wellington, Shropshire.
WN	WOLVERHAMPTON	Bilston Street, Wolverhampton, Staffordshire (1918 -1964).
		Dudley Road, Wolverhampton, Staffordshire.
WR	WORCESTER	Padmore Street, Worcester.
WS	WIGSTON	Station Street, Wigston, Leicestershire.

OTHER CODES

U	Unallocated, area(s) unknown
(P)	Preservation
WDN	Withdrawn

---

* The author wishes to thank Tim Brown, along with The Transport Museum, Wythall, who provided most of this data.
† The code letters for this garage were changed to CH from May 1968. However, for this work CY has been used throughout.

BMMO C5/CM5/CM5T/CS5/C5A

Fleet No.	Registration	Garage Allocations and other details *Reference has been made to specific changes in livery where known.*
4722	722 BHA	**C5,** DH 05/58, store 09/61, DH 03/62, SH 04/63, TH 07/65, store 09/65, LD 04/66, TH 09/66 store 12/66, SA 03/67, SH 05/67, store 09/67, maroon roof 03/68, SH 04/68, store 10/68, DH 04/69, store 09/70, WDN 01/71.
4774	774 GHA	**C5,** BD 08/58, converted to **CS5** 12/61, store 02/62, BD 04/62, OY 05/63, store 12/63, OY 03/64, store 10/65, OY 04/66, store 09/66, OY 03/67, store 10/67, maroon roof 03/68, OY 04/68, store 10/68, OY 04/69, converted to **C5A** 07/69, WDN 02/70.
4775	775 GHA	**C5,** SS 10/58, NN 11/59, SS 04/60, store 02/62, SS 04/62, store 10/62, SA 03/63, SS 04/63, store 12/63, SS 03/64, store 09/65, SS 04/66, store 05/66, converted to **C5A** 08/66, NN 08/66, WDN 10/70.
4776	776 GHA	**C5,** LN 11/58, DY 06/60, store 10/60, DY 04/61, store 10/61, DY 04/62, store 10/62, DY 04/63, store 10/63, DY 03/64, store 10/64, DY 04/65, store 10/65, DY 04/66, converted to **C5A** 09/66, converted for one man operation 01/70, WDN 10/70.
4777	799 GHA	**C5,** SH 12/58, store 10/62, SH 03/63, DH 04/63, converted to **CM5** 05/63, converted to **CS5** ??/63, LD 08/65, converted to **C5A** 07/69, SY 07/69, WDN 10/70.
4778	778 GHA	**C5,** SA 12/58, RY 11/59, DH 10/61, store 02/62, NN 04/62, SS 12/63, NN 03/64, store 09/65, OY 04/66, DH 05/66, store 05/66, converted to **C5A** 07/66, BD 07/66, MN 09/66, BY 07/67, HY 10/69, WDN 12/70.
4779	779 GHA	**C5,** DH 03/59, RY 09/60, converted to **CS5** 12/61, NN 07/62, converted to **CM5** 03/63, store 11/65, converted to **C5A** 02/66, NN 02/66, converted for one man operation 04/70, SS 10/70, WDN 11/70.
4780	780 GHA	**C5,** SN 03/59, store 10/60, SN 04/61, store 10/61, SN 03/62, SH 11/62, store 02/63, EM 04/63, store 10/63, EM 01/64, store 09/65, SH 04/66, store 09/66, SH 03/67, store 10/67, HL 04/68, SH 04/68, store 10/68, SH 12/68, store 12/68, HL 04/69, SE 10/69, store 01/70, OY 05/70, store 09/70, WDN 01/71. Plevey Motor Services, Dudley, 02/71, converted to mobile caravan, 04/71, A. Hawthorn, Sutton Coldfield, (P) 05/98, R. Burdett, Long Eaton, (P) 10/04.
4781	781 GHA	**C5,** WR 03/59, LN 04/60, WR 04/61, store 02/62, MN 04/62, WR 10/62, MN 04/63, store 09/63, MN 03/64, WR 09/64, store 10/64, MN 04/65, store 09/65, MN 04/66, store 05/66, converted to **C5A** 07/66, WR 07/66, MN 05/67, WR 10/69, MN 11/69, converted for one man operation 04/70, WDN 01/71.
4782	782 GHA	**C5,** BE 03/59, store 02/62, BE 04/62, BY 07/65, LN 09/65, store 09/66, LN 10/66, store 10/66, HD 03/67, store 10/68, MN 04/69, store 09/70, WDN 01/71.
4783	783 GHA	**C5,** OY 03/59, store 10/60, OY 04/61, store 10/61, OY 03/62, BD 05/63, store 12/63, BD 03/64, SD 07/65, store 09/65, BD 04/66, store 07/66, converted to **C5A** 08/66, LN 08/66, BY 10/69, converted for one man operation 01/70, WDN 11/70.

A rare picture, taken in early 1958, showing the prototype C5 4722. Note the painted lettering above the side windows. Barrie Smith

A day at the races. Three C5 coaches at Epsom in 1960. 4775 is followed by 4791 and another. Arthur Hustwitt © NA3T

Seen at Bearwood garage in November 1959, left to right, CM5T 4804, C5s 4788 and 4793. Ken Jubb

4784	784 GHA	**C5,** DH 03/59, converted to **CS5** 05/63, store 09/65, DH 04/66, store 10/67, DH 04/68, store 09/70, WDN 01/71.
4785	785 GHA	**C5,** DH 03/59, RY 10/61, converted to **CS5** 12/61, DH 05/62, RH 07/65, BE 09/65, RH 04/66, store 09/66, MN 10/66, store 10/66, RH 03/67, store 09/67, maroon roof 03/68, RH 04/68, store 09/68, WR 02/69, store 09/70, WDN 01/71. L. Margo, International Coach Lines, London SW16, 05/71.
4786	786 GHA	**C5,** DH 03/59, OY 05/60, BD 06/60, store 10/61, BD 03/62, store 02/63, BD 04/63, converted to **CS5** 05/63, DH 07/64, BD 08/64, SD 07/65, store 09/65, SD 04/66, store 10/66, SD 03/67, store 09/67, maroon roof 03/68, SD 04/68, store 09/68, SD 04/69, store 10/69, SD 05/70, store 09/70, WDN 01/71.
4787	787 GHA	**C5,** SA 05/59, CE 04/63, store 09/65, MD 04/66, converted to **C5A** 09/66, CE 09/66, MD 11/67, CE 07/68, converted for one man operation 04/70, WDN 02/71.
4788	788 GHA	**C5,** BD 05/59, OY 06/60, store 02/62, DH 06/62, WL 04/63, store 09/63, WL 03/64, store 09/64, WL 04/65, store 10/65, WL 04/66, store 05/66, converted to **C5A** 07/66, SE 07/66, converted for one man operation 01/70, WDN 11/70.
4789	789 GHA	**C5,** SS 05/59, store 10/65, SS 04/66, converted to **C5A** 09/66, BY 09/66, RY 05/69, converted for one person operation 07/70, WDN 05/71. Office at SW garage 05/71 - 09/73.
4790	790 GHA	**C5,** SA 05/59, RY 09/64, store 09/65, RY 04/66, store 5/66, converted to **C5A** 07/66, SA 07/66, WDN 12/70.
4791	791 GHA	**C5,** WS 05/59, store 09/65, DY 04/66, store 09/66, DY 03/67, store 09/67, maroon roof 04/68, DY 04/68, store 09/68, DY 04/69, OY 03/70, store 09/70, WDN 01/71.
4792	792 GHA	**C5,** LN 05/59, store 02/62, BE 06/62, WR 07/65, BE 04/66, store 07/66, NN 08/66, converted to **C5A** 09/66, SD 09/66, HY 09/66, WDN 01/71.
4793	793 GHA	**C5,** BD 07/59, HD 04/60, store 09/60, HD 04/61, store 10/61, WR 03/62, HD 04/62, store 09/62, WR 03/63, HD 04/63, store 09/63, HD 03/64, store 09/64, HD 04/65, store 10/65, HD 04/66, WR 09/66, SH 06/67, store 10/67, maroon roof 03/68, WR 04/68, store 09/68, DH 04/69, store 01/70, DH 05/70, store 09/70, WDN 01/71.
4794	794 GHA	**C5,** DH 07/59, converted to **CS5** 12/61, SN 05/63, BY 09/65, store 10/65, SN 04/66, store 09/66, KR 03/67, DH 07/67, maroon roof 04/68, store 02/70, converted to **C5A** and one man operation 04/70, KR 05/70, CY 04/71, SD 05/71, WDN 09/71. Plant, Gnosall 11/71, WDN 01/72. Withers Travel, Blackwood 06/72, Pointon, Fenton 09/72, WDN 01/73. Highlander (Sundrive Coaches), Dublin by 09/73, re-registered 5275 ZJ, Keenan, Bullurgan Point, County Louth, derelict by 08/74.
4795	795 GHA	**C5,** DH 08/59, converted to **CS5** 12/61, store 09/65, DH 04/66, CY 05/66, DH 05/66, store 10/66, OY 03/67, EM 06/67, store 10/67, maroon roof 03/68, EM 04/68, store 09/70, WDN 01/71. Hulleys of Baslow (14) 07/71 (licensed 01/72), WDN by 04/73. K. Thompson, Macclesfield 06/73, stock car transporter, Day,Warley, spares 04/76.
4796	796 GHA	**C5,** BD 03/60, converted to **CS5** 05/63, store 10/65, BD 04/66, store 09/66, BD 02/67, store 09/67, maroon roof 04/68, BD 04/68, store 09/68, BD 12/68, store 12/68, BD 04/69, store 02/70, BD 04/70, store 09/70, WDN 01/71.
4797	797 GHA	**C5,** store 02/60, DY 04/60, LN 06/60, store 09/66, LN 03/67, store 09/70, WDN 01/71.
4798	798 GHA	**C5,** store 02/60, SN 04/60, store 02/62, SN 04/62, DH 05/63, BD 07/64, DH 08/64, EM 07/65, LN 01/66, store 02/66, SH 04/66, EM 08/66, converted to **C5A** 09/66, WR 11/68, converted for one man operation 04/70, BY 02/71, WDN 09/71.
4799	799 HHA	**C5,** store 02/60, SE 04/60, store 10/60, SE 04/61, store 10/61, SE 04/62, store 10/62, SE 04/63, store 10/63, SE 03/64, store 10/64, SE 04/65, store 10/65, SE 04/66, store 09/66, SE 03/67, store 09/67, maroon roof 04/68, SE 04/68, store 09/68, CY 04/69, store 09/70, SY 01/71, WDN 12/71.
4800	800 HHA	**CM5,** NN 09/60, store 10/65, converted to **C5A** 01/66, CE 01/66, SS 11/70, WDN 04/71.
4801	801 HHA	**CM5T** BD 11/59, converted to **CS5** with C37F layout 03/65, SA 06/65, DH 06/65, store 10/65, DH 04/66, converted **C5A** 06/66, WS 04/68, converted for one man operated 05/70, NN 10/70, RY 05/71, WDN 08/71. Plant, Gnosall 11/71, Stubbs, Tunstall 03/72, WDN 05/72.
4802	802 HHA	**CM5T,** BD 11/59, converted **CS5** with C37F layout 03/65, OY 03/65, store 10/65, OY 04/66, converted to **C5A** 06/66, WL 09/66, converted for one man operation 03/70, WDN 04/71.
4803	803 HHA	**CM5T,** BD 11/59, store 03/61, converted to C5 with C37F layout 05/61, WS 05/61, store 09/65, WS 11/65, SS 04/66, store 09/66, converted to **C5A** 12/66, WL 01/67, converted for one man operation 03/70, WDN 12/70.
4804	804 HHA	**CM5T,** BD 11/59, store 07/65, converted to **C5A** with C37F layout 12/65, SS 12/65, WDN 09/70.
4805	805 HHA	**CM5,** BD 11/59, converted to **CM5T** with C34F seating layout and toilet 01/60, DH 04/65, converted to **CS5** with C37F layout 05/65, SE 05/65, store 09/65, SE 04/66, store 07/66, converted to **C5A** 08/66, SE 08/66, HL 09/66, converted for one man operation 02/70, DY 10/70, WDN 02/71.

4806	806 HHA	**CM5**, BD 11/59, converted to **CM5T** with C34F seating layout and toilet 04/60, converted to **CS5** 06/65, HL 06/65, store 09/65, converted to **C5A** with C37F layout 03/66, KR 03/66, converted for one man operation 12/69, BY 03/70, WDN 02/71.
4807	807 HHA	**CM5**, BD 11/59, converted to **CM5T** with C34F seating layout and toilet 12/59, converted to **C5A** with C37F layout 04/66, LN 04/66, DH 10/70, WDN 12/70.
4808	808 HHA	**CM5**, BD 11/59, NN 08/60, store 01/66, converted to **C5A** 04/66, SA 04/66, store 06/67, DH 03/68, converted for one man operation 03/70, LN 10/70, WDN 01/71.
4809	809 HHA	**CM5T**, BD 11/59, store 09/65, converted to **C5A** with C37F layout 02/66, TH 02/66, converted for one person operation 03/70, WDN 01/71. Crutchley, Lichfield, mobile film demonstration unit 02/71, Day, Warley, (P) 1976, scrapped.
4810	810 HHA	**CM5T**, BD 11/59, DH 04/65, BD 05/65, store 08/65, converted to **C5A** with C37F layout 03/66, SY 03/66, WDN 01/71.
4811	811 HHA	**CM5T**, BD 07/60, DH 04/65, converted to **CS5** 05/65, WN 05/65, store 10/65, converted to **C5A** with C37F layout 03/66, WR 03/66, converted for one man operation 04/70, WN 01/71, WDN 05/71.
4812	812 HHA	**CM5**, NN 09/60, store 02/66, converted to **C5A** 04/66, WS 04/66, store 06/67, WDN 01/68, accident.
4813	813 HHA	**CM5**, NN 09/60, store 02/66, converted to **C5A** 05/66, SW 05/66, WDN 01/71.
4814	814 HHA	**CM5T**, DH 07/60, BD 07/65, store 07/65, converted to **C5A** with C37F layout 01/66, BY 01/66, LN 04/69, DH 10/70, WDN 12/70.
4815	815 HHA	**CM5T** DH 07/60, store 02/66, converted to **C5A** with C37F layout 04/66, HD 04/66, converted for one man operation 04/70, WDN 02/71.
4816	816 HHA	**C5**, DH 04/61, HY 05/61, store 02/63, HY 04/63, store 09/65, HY 04/66, store 09/66, SW 10/66, store 10/66, SS 03/67, store 09/67, maroon roof 04/68, SS 04/68, store 09/68, SA 03/69, SS 04/69, store 09/70, WDN 01/71. L. Margo, International Coach Lines, London SW16, 05/71.
4817	817 HHA	**C5**, BY 04/61, store 12/61, LN 03/62, BY 04/62, store 10/62, LN 03/63, BY 04/63, EM 11/63, store 11/63, BY 01/64, store 10/64, BY 04/65, store 09/65, converted to **C5A** 01/66, EM 01/66, WR 10/66, converted for one man operation 04/70, MN 05/71, WDN 11/71.
4818	818 HHA	**C5**, KR 04/61, store 10/61, BE 03/62, KR 04/62, store 10/62, KR 03/63, store 10/63, BD 01/64, store 10/64, KR 04/65, store 09/65, KR 04/66, store 05/66, converted to **C5A** 07/66, BE 07/66, KR 09/69, converted for one man operation 01/70, WDN 08/71. G and J Coaches, Gnosall, 09/71, not used, scrapped 04/74.
4819	819 HHA	**C5**, HL 04/61, store 10/61, HL 04/62, store 10/62, HL 04/63, store 10/63, NN 01/64, HL 03/64, store 10/64, HL 04/65, store 10/65, HL 04/66, store 09/66, CY 03/67, SN 05/67, store 10/67, maroon roof 04/68, SN 04/68, store 10/68, LN 03/69, SN 04/69, SD 03/70, SN 04/70, store 09/70, WDN 01/71. The Lichfield Speedway Supporter's Club 02/71, Morris, Tamworth by 02/83, Whitelaw, Sutton Coldfield, unknown date, Thomas, Telford, (P) 06/92. Messrs Duffle, Hatton and Mould, Cannock, (P) 03/99, D. Parry, (P), Warley 03/07.

At the time of the introduction of motorway express services, 4806 was to the 37-seat CM5 configuration, but by April 1960 it had been modified to CM5T standard. Ken Jubb

4816 remained as a standard C5 all of its working life. It is seen at Coventry's Pool Meadow, together with C5A 4801. Patrick Kingston

C5 4825 waits for race going customers on the coach stand in Humberstone Gate, Leicester. Peter Smith/Leicester Transport Heritage Trust

4820	820 HHA	**C5,** CY 04/61, store 10/61, CY 04/62, store 10/62, CY 04/63, store 10/63, SS 01/64, CY 03/64, store 10/64, WN 12/64, CY 04/65, store 09/65, CY 04/66, converted to **C5A** 09/66, WDN 03/71.
4821	821 HHA	**C5,** WR 05/61, store 02/63, WR 04/63, store 10/65, WR 04/66, store 07/66, converted to **C5A** 08/66, HD 08/66, converted for one man operation 03/70, WDN 05/71.
4822	822 HHA	**C5,** EM 06/61, store 02/63, converted to **CM5** 04/63, NN 04/63, store 09/65, converted to **CS5** ??/65, HL 04/66, store 09/66, HL 03/67, store 09/67, HL 04/68, store 09/68, HL 04/69, store 09/70, WDN 01/71.
4823	823 HHA	**C5,** CE 07/61, store 10/61, SS 03/62, CE 04/62, store 02/63, converted to **CM5** 04/63, DH 04/63, converted to **CS5** 05/65, CY 05/65, store 10/65, CY 04/66, store 05/66, converted to **C5A** 05/66, CY 05/66, SY 09/66, WDN 09/71. Plant, Gnosall, spares 10/71.
4824	824 HHA	**C5,** SS 05/61, store 10/65, SS 04/66, MD 09/66, store 10/66, MD 03/67, store 09/67, maroon roof 04/68, MD 04/68, CE 07/68, store 09/68, CE 04/69, store 09/70, SY 01/71, WDN 12/71.
4825	825 HHA	**C5,** SA 05/61, store 02/63, SA 04/63, store 07/66, SY 08/66, store 09/66, SY 03/67, store 10/67, maroon roof 04/68, SY 04/68, store 09/68, SY 04/69, store 09/70, WDN 01/71.
4826	826 HHA	**CM5T,** BD 03/61, converted to **CS5** with C37F layout 03/65, WS 04/65, store 10/65, WS 04/66, store 07/66, converted to **C5A** 08/66, DH 08/66, BD 03/67, converted for one man operation 03/70, LN 10/70, WDN 03/71.
4827	827 HHA	**C5,** DH 05/61, RY 05/62, store 02/63, RY 04/63, SA 09/64, store 10/65, BD 04/66, store 09/66, DH 10/66, store 10/66, BD 03/67, store 10/67, maroon roof 03/68, BD 04/68, store 09/68, BD 12/68, store 12/68, BD 04/69, store 01/70, SH 05/70, store 09/70, WDN 01/71. L. Margo, International Coach Lines, London SW16, 05/71.
4828	828 HHA	**C5,** SW 07/61, store 10/65, SW 04/66, store 05/66, converted to **C5A** 07/66, WS 07/66, SW 09/66, converted for one man operation 05/70, SA 12/70, WDN 09/71. Plant, Gnosall, spares 10/71.
4829	829 HHA	**C5,** DH 07/61, SY 04/63, store 10/63, SY 03/64, store 10/64, SY 04/65, store 10/65, SY 04/66, store 09/66, WS 03/67, store 09/67, WS 04/68, store 09/68, SS 03/69, WS 04/69, store 09/69, converted to **C5A** and one man operation 03/70, KR 03/70, WDN 09/71. Office at DY garage 10/71 - 03/73.
4830	830 HHA	**CM5T,** DH 05/61, store 09/66, DH 05/67, store 09/67, DH 05/68, store 09/68, DH 05/69, store 09/70, DH 05/71, store 09/71, WDN 07/72. Used from time to time as the Directors' coach between 1961 – 1967. Longbridge Engineering, Bromsgrove 11/72. Mr. McGlone, Willis, Michigan, U.S.A., mobile caravan 01/73.
4831	831 HHA	**C5,** SY 07/61, store 10/61, SY 04/62, store 10/62, converted to **CM5** 04/63, NN 04/63, WR 11/65, DH 03/66, store 05/66, converted to **C5A** 05/66, SS 05/66, WDN 10/70.
4832	832 HHA	**C5,** WL 08/61, store 09/61, WL 04/62, store 09/62, converted to **CM5** 04/63, NN 04/63, WR 11/65, store 04/66, converted to **C5A** 05/66, RY 05/66, converted for one man operation 05/70, WDN 01/71.
4833	833 HHA	**C5,** WN 08/61, store 12/61, converted to **CM5** 07/62, WR 07/62, store 01/66, converted to **C5A** 05/66, DH 05/66, TH 09/66, converted for one man operation ??/70, LD 03/71, WDN 05/71.

Coaches were often de-licenced during the winter months. Not so for C5 4829, pictured on a private hire to a colliery in February 1962.
Ken Jubb

4834	834 HHA	**C5,** BE 09/61, store 05/62, converted to **CM5** 07/62, WR 07/62, store 03/66, converted to C5A 05/66, KR 05/66, converted for one man operation 05/70, WDN 02/71.
4835	835 HHA	**C5,** store 11/61, converted to **CM5** 07/62, RY 07/62, WR 07/62, store 04/66, converted to C5A 05/66, WL 05/66, LD 03/67, converted for one man operation 03/70, WDN 03/71.
4836	836 HHA	**C5,** DH 10/61, store 05/62, converted to **CM5** 07/62, DH 07/62, store 06/65, converted to C5A 05/66, MN 05/66, SH 10/69, HY 12/70, WDN 03/71. L. Margo, International Coach Lines, London SW16, 07/71, scrapped 06/72.
4837	837 HHA	**C5,** BD 11/61, store 03/62, converted to **CM5** 07/62, DH 07/62, RY 01/63, NN 04/65, store 12/65, converted to **CS5** 03/66, WN 04/66, store 09/66, WN 03/67, store 09/67, maroon roof 03/68, WN 04/68, store 09/68, WN 04/69, store 09/70, WDN 01/71.

BMMO CM6/CM6T/CM6A

Fleet No.	Registration	Garage Allocations and other details
		Reference has been made to specific changes in livery where known.

5295	5495 HA	**CM6T,** DH 03/63, BD 06/63, RY 02/65, WS 06/70, store 10/70, WS 04/71, NN 11/71, store 09/72, WDN 03/73.
5646	BHA 646C	**CM6T,** BD 02/65, store 09/71, WDN 07/72.
5647	BHA 647C	**CM6T,** BD 04/65, maroon roof 01/68, store 03/72, WDN 07/72.
5648	BHA 648C	**CM6T,** BD 04/65, maroon roof 01/68, store 10/70, BD 04/71, store 03/72, *modified externally with larger destination display and waistrail brightwork 05/72*, BD 05/72, CY 12/73, WDN 04/74.
5649	BHA 649C	**CM6T,** BD 04/65, maroon roof 01/68, store 10/70, BD 03/71, store 03/72, WDN 07/72.
5650	BHA 650C	**CM6T,** BD 04/65, maroon roof 05/67, store 03/72, *modified externally with larger destination display and waistrail brightwork 05/72*, BD 05/72, *painted National white livery 12/72*, CY 12/73, WDN 04/74.
5651	BHA 651C	**CM6T,** DH 05/65, RY 08/66, DH 10/66, maroon roof 02/68, store 09/71, *modified externally with larger destination display and waistrail brightwork 03/72*, DH 04/72, *painted National white livery 01/74*, WDN 04/74.
5652	BHA 652C	**CM6T,** DH 06/65, *modified externally with larger destination display and waistrail brightwork 05/72*, *painted National white livery 06/72*, WDN 04/74.
5653	BHA 653C	**CM6T,** DH 05/65, maroon roof 01/68, store 09/71, *modified externally with larger destination display and waistrail brightwork 03/72*, BD 05/72, DH 12/73, WDN 04/74.
5654	BHA 654C	**CM6T,** BD 06/65, store 03/71, converted to **CM6A** with C46F seating and one man operation, one piece driver operated entrance door and larger destination blind 05/71, WR 05/71, store 09/71, re-classified **CM6** upon removal of one man operation equipment 05/72, BD 05/72, *painted National white livery 12/73 (but not modified externally with waistrail brightwork)*, CY 12/73, U 04/74, WDN 09/74.
5655	BHA 655C	**CM6T,** BD 07/65, maroon roof 02/68, store 05/72, WDN 07/72.
5656	BHA 656C	**CM6T,** BD 09/65, maroon roof 09/67, *modified externally with larger destination display and waistrail brightwork*, *painted National white livery 11/72*, CY 12/73, U 05/74, WDN 09/74. Midland Red Preservation Society, Leamington, (P) 08/75, BaMMOT, Wythall, (P) 05/78.
5657	BHA 657C	**CM6T,** BD 09/65, maroon roof 09/67, *modified externally with larger destination display and waistrail brightwork*, *painted National white livery 08/72*, CY 12/73, WDN 04/74.
5658	BHA 658C	**CM6T,** NN 10/65, BD 11/70, store 09/71, DH 11/71, BD 04/72, *painted National white livery 07/72, (but not modified externally with larger destination display and waistrail brightwork)*, 12/73, WDN 04/74.
5659	BHA 659C	**CM6T,** BD 10/65, DH 09/66, maroon roof 02/68, BD 04/72, DH 02/73, *painted National white livery 06/73 (but not modified externally with larger destination display and waistrail brightwork)*, WDN 04/74.
5660	DHA 960C	**CM6T,** NN 11/65, maroon roof 02/68, store 09/71, *modified externally with larger destination display and waistrail brightwork 01/72*, NN 04/72, *painted National white livery 11/73*, WDN 04/74.
5661	DHA 961C	**CM6T,** NN 11/65, maroon roof 03/68, BD 11/70, NN 04/71, store 09/71, *modified externally with larger destination display and waistrail brightwork 02/72*, NN 04/72, WDN 04/74.
5662	DHA 962C	**CM6T,** NN 12/65, maroon roof 06/67, BD 03/72, NN 09/72, *modified externally with larger destination display and waistrail brightwork*, *painted National white 01/73*, WDN 04/74. Morris, Pencoed, 06/75, WDN 11/75. Everton, Droitwich (loan) 03/76, WDN 06/76. J. Dauncey, Bromsgrove, mobile caravan 12/77, BaMMOT Wythall, spares 02/84, Chris Hatton, Norton Canes, (P) 01/00.

5663	DHA 963C	**CM6T,** NN 12/65, maroon roof 06/67, WS 06/70, NN 04/71, *modified externally with larger destination display and waistrail brightwork, painted National livery 10/72,* WDN 04/74. Turriff (contractor) (loan) 06/75, Catterall Coaches, Southam 07/75, Morris, Pencoed, 09/75, WDN 11/75. Everton, Droitwich (loan) 03/76, WDN 06/76.
5664	DHA 964C	**CM6T,** NN 01/66, maroon roof 07/67, BD 03/72, store 09/72, *modified externally with larger destination display and waistrail brightwork, painted National white 01/73,* BD 02/73, CY 12/73, WDN 04/74.
5665	DHA 965C	**CM6T,** NN 01/66, maroon roof 07/67, store 10/71, *modified externally with larger destination display and waistrail brightwork 03/72,* BD 04/72, NN 01/73, *painted National white 05/73,* DH 05/73, U 05/74, WDN 09/74.
5666	EHA 666D	**CM6T,** NN 02/66, maroon roof 07/67, store 10/70, NN 04/71, *modified externally with larger destination display and waistrail brightwork, painted National white livery 02/73,* DH 05/73, WDN 04/74
5667	EHA 667D	**CM6,** WR 03/66, maroon roof 08/67, DH 03/72, *painted National white livery 10/73 (but not modified externally with larger destination display and waistrail brightwork),* U 11/73, WDN 09/74.
5668	EHA 668D	**CM6,** WR 03/66, maroon roof 02/68, DH 03/72, *modified externally with larger destination display and waistrail brightwork, painted National white livery 03/73,* NN 05/73, WDN 04/74.
5669	EHA 669D	**CM6,** WR 04/66, maroon roof 03/68, NN 03/72, store 01/73, WDN 03/73.
5670	EHA 670D	**CM6,** WR 04/66, DH 08/66, RY 09/66, WR 09/66, maroon roof 05/67, NN 03/72, *modified externally with larger destination display and waistrail brightwork, painted National white livery 05/73,* WDN 04/74.
5671	EHA 671D	**CM6,** DH 05/66, WR 08/66, RY 09/66, maroon roof 07/67, SA 05/69, RY 06/70, WDN 03/73
5672	EHA 672D	**CM6T,** DH 05/66, maroon roof 01/68, store 09/72, WDN 03/73.
5673	EHA 673D	**CM6T,** DH 05/66, maroon roof 04/68, store 04/73, WDN 12/73.
5674	EHA 674D	**CM6T,** DH 05/66, maroon roof 03/68, store 10/71, *modified externally with larger destination display and waistrail brightwork 05/72,* DH 05/72, *painted National white 09/73,* WDN 04/74

Opposite page:

The driver of CM6T (prototype) 5295 executes a tight turn as he manoeuvres out of Bearwood garage. Ken Jubb

This page:

Top: **CM6T 5656 was on a private charter ferrying prisoners from Winson Green Prison to the County Court at Warwick in July 1973.** Patrick Kingston

Centre: **CM6Ts 5657 and 5663 at Pool Meadow, Coventry, in 1969.** T W Moore

Bottom left: **CM6T 5663 spent a few weeks with contractor, Turriff, and was caught here in Leamington Spa in June 1975.** Transport Museum, Wythall collection

Bottom right: **A former Worcester CM6 that went to Nuneaton was 5670. The garage appears to have favoured these vehicles for non-motorway work, this one being on a private charter.** Photobus

Acknowledgements

In addition to those whose names appear in the text and in photo credits, the author wishes to thank the following for their assistance so generously given: Andrew Hawthorn, Brian Dicks, Christopher Davis, David Hayward, Dick Nutt, Gareth Jones, Gavin Booth, Geoff Price, Keith Lloyd, Martin Fisher, Martin Hobson, Mick Loon, Mike Greenwood, Rod Bates, Roy Finney, Tim Brown, The Kithead Trust and The Transport Museum, Wythall (especially Dave Taylor, Malcolm Keeley, Mike Jordan, Paul Gray). On the production side: Bill Gladstone, Dave Heaney, David Oliver, John Barclay, John Hobday, John Taylor, Neil Lewis and Tony Mitchell.

This project is very much a family effort; thank you to my wife Carole and daughters Emma and Julie.

Bibliography

BBC History magazine: November 2009.
Bus & Coach: November 1959 and May 1961.
Buses: M1 Commemoration by Stewart J Brown; Ian Allan, February 1990.
Characters of the Bus Industry: Ted Gadsby; Article on D M Sinclair, The Omnibus Society 2004.
Classic Bus: Alan Townsin; Two-part article on D M Sinclair, issues 1 and 2 1992.
Design and Operation of Motorway Coaches: J Pearson; The Institution of Mechanical Engineers, March 1962.
Midland Red Allocations Fleetlist, 1946-1972: Tim Brown; BaMMOT, 2008.
Midland Red Net: http://midlandred.net/fleet/bmmo/c5/index.shtml.
Midland Red Staff Bulletin: various issues, 1959-1962.
Midland Red, A History of the Company and its vehicles from 1940 to 1970: Paul Gray, Malcolm Keeley, John Seale; The Transport Publishing Company, 1979.
MIRA – Fifty Years of Excellence: written and compiled by Dick Stirley and Keith Read; Atalink Project Ltd, London, 1996.
Passenger Transport: 17th August 1960.
The Commercial Motor: 27th November 1959 and 16th March 1962.
The Motor: 20th April 1960.
The Transport Journal: 6th November 1959.

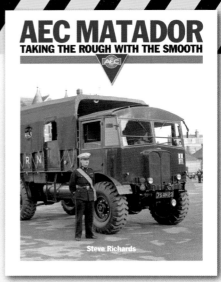